D0719293

SCOTLAND
THROUGH AMERICAN EYES

TO THE

PEOPLE OF SCOTLAND

SCOTLAND
THROUGH AMERICAN EYES

BY

ROBERT SCOTT

". . . the northern sister fair,
That hath the heath-bells in her blowing hair."

EDINBURGH: T. & T. CLARK
1928

Printed in Great Britain
by Turnbull & Spears, Edinburgh

PREFACE

My prolonged stay within these hospitable shores tempted me to redeem the time—to buy up, as it were, the opportunity of studying Scotland past and present, and from as many angles as possible.

To see the soul of an old country through the soul of a much younger country, the United States of America, a country unhampered by antiquated and anomalous institutions like feudalism, the hereditary principle, and a State-supported Church, has some distinct advantages; and these advantages are enhanced when we consider America's freedom from the policy of Imperialism, European controversies, and a weighty body of traditional ideas. It frequently happens that those who are too close to a given situation are apt to see it from only one side, the side nearest to them. To complete the picture a presentation of the far-off view is necessary.

My more than forty years' residence in the United States of America, frequent visits to the scenes of the old land during that long period, and a variety of experiences during the last fifteen months in touring anew the land of my birth, has made it possible for me to attempt the task of combining the near and the distant view, considering and commenting on most of the aspects of national life in a studious, if not exhaustive, way. While all the subjects relating to national life could not be fully treated within reasonable limits, enough had to be carefully considered in order to get a due sense of proportion.

What I have endeavoured to do in these pages is to give a compact and, I trust, impartial study, a sort of appraisal or auditing of the chief elements in the national life covering the last fifty to sixty years, noting the gains, the drawbacks, and the losses as the case may be. In this agreeable occupation and in this chivalrous atmosphere I have been

> A chield's amang you takin' notes
> And faith he'll prent it.

The governing motive in all that is said has been to see things just as they are so that some steady advancement may be made towards what they ought to be. Criticism, of course, was unavoidable, but it is of a constructive and friendly nature. It is even mellowed by the fact that I have associated myself with some of the judgments given. There are a few suggestions humbly submitted, and into the entire study there is woven some of my own philosophy.

An untold amount of Scottish literature had to be read in the course of my study and travels. I take this opportunity of tendering my sincere thanks to the many

Scottish authors whose works I have consulted.

Two services I wish to acknowledge with appreciation and thanks: first, that of Mr Robert Adams, Assistant City Librarian, The Mitchell Library, Glasgow, for reading the proofs during my absence from Scotland; and the other is the excellent work done by Miss H. H. Harkness, also of The Mitchell Library, in preparing the copy for the printer.

GLASGOW, *January* 1928

CONTENTS

SCOTLAND
THROUGH AMERICAN EYES

CHAPTER I

INTRODUCTORY

Beauty dwells in the soul of the beholder.

WHILE waiting leisurely for the luncheon announcement at a small hotel located in one of the villages in the Shetland Isles my eyes feasted on a choice bit of sea and landscape. A sunny June day made the view all the more impressive. From my vantage point the foreground was an unruffled loch with but a solitary and tiny sail-boat moving very slowly. On the other side of the loch there was the green sloping land almost touching the peaceful water, and near the top of the brae a wee and newly white-washed cottage. The absence of trees and shrubbery, the loneliness and simplicity of the situation, all combined to form what seemed to me a restful picture, just what is so frequently needed preparatory to a midday meal. What is the good of admiring and enjoying something if one cannot share it with others ? So this is what the charming scene evoked—Isn't that a beautiful little picture ?

Standing by my side was a mature university gentleman from England. He instantly took exception to my æsthetic judgment by remarking : "It is not beauty you see ; what you are thinking about is sentiment." Without entering into the details of the colloquy that ensued, I noticed that my rather cantankerous critic failed to make his appearance at the luncheon table, while I was rewarded by dwelling for long after on the place of sentiment in human affairs. It plays a large and renewing role in the lives of many persons in nearly all lands, and because it does I thought this would be an appropriate place to refer to it. The feeling that is created by certain objects in the homeland, the cluster of pleasant memories slumbering in the nook of every heart, only requires the proper occasion to bring them, as it were, to the surface. It is just deep answering to deep.

Sentiment is often particularly strong among Scotsmen resident in distant parts of the world. Much of this fine soul quality, this strong attachment to the scenes of earlier days, may be attributed in the first place to the unusual physical features of the land. Its mountain settings, its lofty and heathery hills, its attractive glens, its numerous rivers and varied lochs, all combine to make it an enviable land to visit. Alongside of its rugged physical features there is the memory of a somewhat rigorous climate, and very often an impoverished soil with all the attendant struggles and hardships associated with these. From the mere external things we turn to the internal, and there is the memory of the protracted, severe, and persistent struggle for independence and freedom. All these are interwoven in the national character. They find expression in her heroic sons, in her melodious and world-renowned songs, and in her wealth of literature. The national bard sees all nature vibrating and aflame with beauty:

> Wherever I wander, wherever I rove,
> The hills of the Highlands for ever I love.

Dr Sutherland says:

> Every hill is clothed in story,
> Every glen is holy ground.

Henry Drummond, who was born in Stirling in 1851, made this remark to his brother after he had returned from one of his extended trips: "Man, there is no place like this, no place like Scotland." [1]

[1] From *Life of Henry Drummond*, by Principal Sir G. Adam Smith.

Introductory

It is said of a Highland piper during the world war, who, though wounded three times, persisted in carrying on and playing his pipes until he fell mortally wounded : " He knew he was dying — just before his spirit passed away he whispered, ' Oh, if I could only see the high hills again before I die.' "

It cannot be too often repeated that those who were fortunate enough to be brought up and educated in the country owe more to their environment (especially surroundings where there are mountains, hills, glens, lochs, and streams) than is usually credited to this source.

Tennyson, in that memorable little gem on the flower in the crannied wall, says :

Little flower—if I could but understand
What you are, root and all, and all in all,
I should know what man and God is.

This scarcely harmonises with our scientific philosophy. To "know what man and God is," we need to turn to something greater than the flower which has no existence apart from man and God. We can only know mankind in the different stages of his evolution by studying man. With this thought in mind we desire to traverse over, say, fifty or sixty years of Scottish life to discover, if possible, the progress made in that period. The study will take the form of a brief national stocktaking, as it were, not simply quoting figures as an evidence of progress, but endeavouring to get at the deeper values which make for stability, worth, and permanence.

There are some writers who contend that progress is undemonstrable. They claim that better working and living conditions, more lucrative employment, more pleasurable life, and all the benefits science has brought to mankind during the last half century, does not necessarily make for real happiness, for a higher type of men and women. In other words,

Introductory

the claim is made that progress is a matter of the spirit.

At this point a pertinent question would be : Have we not been too partial and provincial in defining the operations of the spirit of God ? The position taken in these pages is, that the operations of the spirit are not confined to any one aspect or department of life. Science and art in all its various forms, no less than religion, indeed all that ministers to the highest needs and ends of human life, breathe and express the spirit of God. To make our point concrete we would here refer to one aspect of life where this spirit is more in evidence than ever before, that is, in the cultivation of the international mind and the steady growth of world unity.

In order to get a clear perspective of the period to be covered, there can scarcely be any question as to the need of knowing something concerning what happened in the past so that the country

19

as a whole may be guided in its plans and purposes for the future. The only question is how far we should go back in the pages of the national life to get an intelligent idea of the causes at work and the effects produced, and at the same time note whatever gains and losses there may be. To meet this difficulty we will content ourselves by noting briefly some of the outstanding facts and events in the early history of the land. They will be, as it were, lighthouses on the way; after that we will confine our study to the period within the memory of those now living.

Before entering on this aspect of our study, a brief reference ought to be made to the physical features of the land, for they form quite a factor in determining the nature of the occupation within the land, and equally so in moulding the character of the people.

Scotland has three distinct geographical regions : (1) the Highlands (the abode

of the Picts); (2) the Central Plain, or
Lowlands; and (3) the Southern Highlands. The main features are its mountains, hills, valleys, and lochs. A glance
at the west coast-line of Scotland, with
its striking irregularity, is a decided contrast to the regularity of the east coast.
Part of the unevenness of the west coast
may point back to a remote period when
a terrific volcanic upheaval visited this
part of the world, changing both topog-
raphy and climate. Whenever or wherever this takes place a change in the
occupations and character of the people
is inevitable. The absence of mineral
wealth and the impoverished condition
of the soil in the Highlands has made
the breeding of stock, the pursuit of
game, and fishing, about the only de-
pendable things. In the Lowlands an
abundance of coal, iron, and lime are to
be found. It is this region which has
contributed most to the prosperity of
the country.

As for the scenery of the land, who that has travelled east and west, north and south, can ever forget its beauties. Queen Victoria, writing the King of the Belgians in June 1865, says: " How delightful it would be to show you our beloved Balmoral, with its glorious scenery and heavenly air, its solitude and absence of all contact with the mere miserable frivolities and worldlinesses of this wicked world! The mountains seem fresh from God's hand, nearer to Heaven, and the primitive people to have *kept* that chivalrous loyalty and devotion—*seen* hardly, indeed *now nowhere*, else ! " [1]

While the writer does not share this reflection on the world we live in, few would disagree with its warm appreciation of the Highlands.

The story of a people may, in part, be likened to a great stream. It is something very real and full of life.

[1] In *The Letters of Queen Victoria* (1862–1878), edited by George E. Buckle.

Introductory

There is the rise, the even and uneven flow of the river out into the larger life of the ocean. The stream which we are to trace in outline had its rise long before Agricola entered North Britain in A.D. 80. But that part antedating this time is practically unknown to us. But we do know that for about three hundred years the Romans traversed and occupied the land lying largely to the south of the Forth and Clyde rivers. This conquest is said to have reached the borderland of the Highlands. No stream is without its moods, and the same may be said of the people of a country. The Roman invasion under Agricola represented the military aspect of life, aggression and conquest, while St Ninian in the fourth century and St Columba and St Kentigern in the sixth century represent the religious aspect, peace and unity. Outwardly these early missionaries were unlike John the Baptist, but they were like him in the spirit that moved them, in that they were preparing the way for a new and better order of things. The Baptist preached to Jews. These later evangelists had a much more diversified congregation—Celts, Britons, Picts, and Scots. It is an absorbing study in the history of nations to note the many different kinds of walls there are that separated and do now separate peoples. It was a massive Roman wall which separated the Romans from the Celts in these early days in Scotland. It was the wall of barbarism and the religion of fear which the pioneers and evangelists had to overcome. To-day, the wall is not military nor barbaric but sternly economic. In the evolution of national life all these steps indicate a clear gain. When a nation is able to make force and selfish power take a subordinate place, and the tendency toward co-operation a larger place, one need not despair of still greater achievements. Of course the withdrawal of the Romans in the fifth century and the incoming of another and very different spirit, manifested in the arduous work of the evangelists, did not mean for Scotland the cessation of strife and war. What the Romans left unfinished and unconquered of northern territory soon became the battleground of the different tribes and peoples that were in that part of the country. There were the Picts— said to be the earliest race of which there is any record; the Scots of Celtic origin who hailed from Ireland in the sixth century; the Cymrie, that is the Welsh; and finally the Teutons. One can easily imagine at this early date how the lust for power and territory aided and prolonged the strife and brutal warfare, just as later on in the history of the land Scottish kings "had done all they could to stir up strife between the different clans. They had granted the same lands to different chiefs." [1] But we do not

[1] From *The Macleods of Dunvegan*, 1927. (Privately printed.)

have to travel very far to find a historical reference to a characteristic which has remained through all the centuries the predominant note in the life of the Scottish people—religion. Bede, writing at the beginning of the eighth century, says: " This island at the present time contains five nations, the Angles, Britons, Scots, Picts, and Latins, each in its own dialect cultivating one and the same sublime study of divine truth—the Latin tongue by the study of the Scriptures has become common to all the rest." This study unquestionably helped to prepare the way for the union of the Picts and Scots and the establishment of one kingdom in the same century. This union may be said to be prophetic, for have we not here in embryo the unconscious working out of one of those great universal truths which is much in evidence in our own time—world-unity. Here it may be said that at no time in the varied active life of old Scotland did she ever stand alone.

Introductory

Foreign culture and commerce and adventure have left their impress on the character of the people. The early stage of the national life may be termed the age of conquest. Admitting that the military force was very much in the foreground in these days, its powers waned as the centuries passed, and religion became the country's chief distinctive feature and also her greatest asset. The study of the Scriptures (in the Latin tongue) had a marked effect on the life of the people. It practically paved the way for a united kingdom, something which was then foreign to militarism.

About the year 802 Dunkeld, instead of Iona, became the religious centre. But Iona to-day is still the Mecca for hundreds who journey there each year to pay homage to St Columba. Dunkeld became a common meeting-place for the peoples of kindred blood, who had fought each other for centuries. The Danes and the Norsemen landed on the western coast about this time. Their coming doubtless infused new life into the people. In 843 the Dalriada Scots conquered the Southern Picts, and it was in this same century that Scotland was united under the government of one king—Kenneth. Two centuries later the country was nominally Christian. There were some real constructive forces at work about this period; the reign of David I. (1124–1153) and Alexander II. and III. (1214–1286) may be cited as such. It is often a difficult matter to say definitely when one age ends and another begins. To say, for example, that the age of conquest had spent itself at this time would be incorrect. We are, however, on sure ground when we affirm that a new age had begun. The work of consolidation is now an actuality, and it is in this age we discern the foundation for a national consciousness. Individualism and physical prowess counted for much in those days, but it was beginning to count for less.

Introductory

Suppose there had been no Battle of Bannockburn in 1314, would there have been any independence for Scotland or any Scottish Parliament at Cambuskenneth Abbey in 1326 ? Severe as were her battles with England from the eleventh to the sixteenth centuries, and dastardly as were the court intrigues which played havoc with her commerce, the century following Bannockburn finds her active in educational work. Three of her four universities were founded in the fifteenth century, and this was followed by a period of commercial development. During the reign of James IV. (1488–1513) printing was introduced, and it was in the time of James IV. that we get the poems of William Dunbar and Gavin Douglas.

The emergence of a people from one condition to something higher is usually of a piecemeal character. In the nature of the case it could not be otherwise. The stream has its variations, its days of evenness and unevenness, and this is what we find in Scotland about this time. On the one hand we see the founding of her universities, on the other we find The Scottish Estates successful in passing a law for the burning of heretics. It is just about four centuries ago (1528) that Patrick Hamilton, a poor martyr of the Scottish Reformation, was burned at St Andrews for heresy. A man's soul could scarcely be called his own then. We have improved since then, but is it not true that there are literally thousands of men to-day burdened with the shackles of denominational doctrines?

It is never too late to pay a tribute to those who dared be true to their convictions and vision. In the great uphill fight against the Sovereign it was the men of the Patrick Hamilton and George Wishart type in the homeland, and Knox, Luther, and Calvin in foreign lands, that hastened the coming of the Reformation in Scotland. About fifteen years after the burning of Hamilton, an

Act was passed permitting the general use of the Bible in the vernacular.

The Reformation (1559), followed by the action of the General Assembly in 1573 and in 1581, making Presbytery and not Episcopacy the policy of the National Church, was the dawn of a new and brighter day for Scotland. It was the unloosing of the soul of a brave people, and the leave-taking of an ecclesiastical system that was a veritable millstone. It was the national consciousness asserting itself. For that period in the history of the national life it was, in a sense, a fulfilment of a prophetic note struck over two thousand years ago " let justice roll down as waters and righteousness as an everflowing stream."

The forces which brought about the Reformation were not only religious, they were social and economic also. At a time when the entire population of Scotland did not exceed a million, slumdom, in some of its worst forms, was not unknown. Social conditions had reached the breaking point, "mair they could not thole." In the following century Burns wrote these lines :

> An' when the gentry's life I saw,
> What way poor bodies liv'd ava.
> Our laird gets in his racked rents,
> His coals, his kane, an' a' his stents.

Henrysone, writing of conditions then, said : " The worst wolves are lords that have lands as a loan from God, and set them to ' maillaris ' or ' rentallers.' Then they vex the tenant ere half the term be gone ' with pykit quarrels ' for to make ' him flitt ' [remove] ' or pay the gersum ' [grassum] ' new agane.' "

Why should one wonder that Socialism and Communism have taken root on these shores ?

The course of a nation's life is sometimes deflected by seemingly insignificant matters. No one knows what would have happened to the religious life of

Scotland had Knox not been driven to Switzerland. The type of theology then imported was perhaps the only brand available, and at the same time may have fitted the particular needs of the period and the conceptions of life then prevalent.

In pre- and post-Reformation days religious instruction was given by the Church. The burden of the instruction was not so much for guidance and helpfulness in the active affairs of the next day or week, but mainly preparation for the next world. It was religious exhortation and teaching at long range, and, being so, failed to hit the mark.

It was in 1592, just one hundred years after the discovery of America, that Parliament declared Presbyterianism to be the polity of the Church of Scotland. The new creed and polity were regarded as divine in their origin. Firm in this belief, one can well imagine the feelings and temper of the people of the new Church towards those sovereigns

Scotland through American Eyes

that reigned in post-Reformation times;
sovereigns out of sympathy with the
convictions and wishes of those who
belonged to the new order. The hostility
of the rulers was strangely matched by a
severity and arbitrariness on the part of
the people in an effort to make the new
creed compulsory on all. If those who
represented the people could arrogate
to themselves divine right for a creed,
why should not kings exercise a like
privilege for something which they considered important ? Just a little over a
hundred years from the Reformation this
did come to pass. Charles II. insisted
that he had the divine right to impose
his will on the people, and James VI.
insisted upon his famous *Five Articles*
being carried out. Here is " anise and
cummin " with a vengeance ! Communi-
cants were required to adopt the kneeling
instead of the sitting posture; Easter
and Christmas were to be observed;
confirmation was introduced; the com-

munion could be administered in the
house to the dying, and baptism must
be on the first Sunday after the child's
birth. This was enough to strain the
loyalty of any people. What an attractive subject this would be for a skilful
and imaginative artist! It might be
called the " Clash of Authority, Church
versus State." Both took refuge in the
same conception and the same source.
To which court of appeal could they go
to settle the matter ? Certainly in such
a controversy the parties concerned could
not be the judges of their own views
and actions, so the matter was allowed
to await developments. The controversy
was finally settled by the Revolution of
1689. Something analogous to this old
controversy is going on in Scotland to-day
regarding the proper observance of the
Sabbath. Those who speak and write
for the Church of Scotland largely insist
on obedience to the Fourth Commandment—divine authority again. A con-

siderable number of people, on the other hand, incline to give a more liberal interpretation of what they think is best for man, basing their opinion on the new and vastly different conditions of life now prevailing from what existed when the commandments were promulgated. Whenever or wherever that view is honestly entertained it is clothed with just as much authority as the Fourth Commandment. On the ground that both parties are sincere and intent on what is best for the community, both may be said to be divinely moved. The Church is practically confined to but one aspect of life, namely, religion. The State, on the other hand, has to do with numerous interests such as health, education, industry, commerce, recreation, the making of highways, the making and administering of laws, and so on, thus representing more varied interests in the life of the individual than the Church. This widening of interests, like that of commerce and industry, unquestionably, in the course of time, has lessened the influence of the Church. What seems to be in process of becoming a reality is something like this. The dividing line between Church and State is much less marked than formerly. What was once regarded as secular and sacred, material and spiritual, is now denominated not so much by any one of these terms but by what is, under the circumstances, considered the best for the individual at the present time. That which ministers to the highest interests and ends of the individual, regardless of whether the Church or the State is the agent of the ministration, may rightly be said to be spiritual. This is only emphasising a general truth which coincides with New Testament and twentieth-century thought.

Looking back at the introduction of Calvinism into Scotland, one must be considerate of the times. Religion, as then and now conceived, is as different as night is from day. With our larger experience, wider diffusion of knowledge, and entirely new conditions, our views must undergo some change. Hence, we would not do now what was then done by the State, sanction a given creed and polity for the nation. What was then done deliberately had to be undone gradually—unloose men and women from the imposition of prescribed dogmas. While the Presbyterian Church was good enough for many it did not meet the requirements of all, for the Episcopalians in large numbers refused to identify themselves with the Established Church.

During the period between the Reformation and the Revolution, individualism was powerful, as was ecclesiasticism and dogma; so were strife and schism. When a programme of divine right for a particular theology or polity is insisted on it does not take long before the particular doctrines become trouble-breeders.

Very much depended on the Church

in those days in forwarding the educational life of the community. She was particularly active in getting the different sections in the land to recognise the common interests of all, that infinitely more was to be gained by keeping together than living and working apart.

The population of Scotland at the time of the Union of the Crowns in 1603 numbered less than a million. Big enterprises have little difficulty in almost swallowing little ones, and big countries seldom leave the smaller ones as strong as they were before the amalgamation. Scotland may justly be put in that category.

The year 1688 brought about the Revolution in Scotland. It was in that year that William of Orange came forward as Scotland's deliverer. Two years later the Westminster Confession was ratified by Parliament and Presbytery declared to be the polity of the Church and to be so recognised by the State.

Glasgow, which has now a population of over 1,100,000, had at that time only 30,000, and Edinburgh, with its present population of nearly half a million, had then only 60,000.

The year 1706 witnessed the last session of the Scottish Parliament. Whatever the losses were through the Union of the Parliaments of England and Scotland in 1707, it certainly brought additional strength to the forces of Protestantism and made for spiritual unity. On the other hand, there is ground for the statement made by Lockhart that the 30th April 1707 " was the last day Scotland was Scotland." The truth of this declaration is evident in the Scotland of to-day. Viewed on the whole, we think that both in the development of her commercial life and her language she has lost ground. The language of a country cannot be sacrificed without loss. It is true that the immediate effect was good, for the country, about the middle of the eighteenth century, was moving apace intellectually and industrially as other countries in Europe were. A change of customs and methods naturally came with a change of language, and this change of the smaller for the greater is now felt as it could not be felt when the Union took place.

The Bank of Scotland was founded in 1695, just one year later than the founding of the Bank of England. To-day, nearly all the big banks in Scotland are greatly influenced, if not dominated, by the leading banks in England. There is no quicker and surer way for a people to lose its individuality than by economic pressure. On the other hand, one might cite what happened in the shipbuilding area of Glasgow as an evidence of prosperity and consequence of the Union. It was in 1718 that the first ship built in Glasgow crossed the Atlantic. In 1740 there were 67 vessels which she owned, and in 1792 the number reached 718.

But here is a rather remarkable social and industrial situation. Between the two dates just mentioned everything seems to be going on smoothly in the industrial area, that is, in the Clyde valley, whereas in the northern and western section of the country, where they depended on agriculture, stock raising, and fishing, there is every sign of adversity. It is stated that between 1763 and 1765 thirty thousand Highlanders left their homes for America. It would seem as though there is a profound lesson underlying these dissimilar conditions in the same country. Is it not to be found in the lack of proportion of the various industries ? When the craft industry is almost the exclusive one, top-heavy we might say, and the agricultural industry (which is the chiefest of all) is practically negligible, there is no possible way of escaping the blight of unemployment and serious business depressions.

As Scotland in her very limited

area became highly industrialised in the eighteenth century there came a consequent narrowing of the Church's former power and influence, and a broadening of the entire life of the people. Then, of course, there was a real loss of power from the days when she controlled education, now passed over to the State. Educationally speaking Scotland was strong both at home and abroad. During the eighteenth and nineteenth centuries her commercial and industrial life reached the high-water mark.

In 1829 the population was about 2,360,000 and there were only about 3000 electors.

In 1843 one of the great events in the life of the Scottish people took place. In May of that year 451 members left the Established Church and formed a new organisation, the Free Church of Scotland. In 1904 the Free Church and the United Presbyterian Churches of Scotland sank their differences and joined forces in the United Free Church of Scotland, and at no distant date we may look for the union of the Church of Scotland and the United Free Church.

THE RELIGIOUS LIFE

CHAPTER II

THE RELIGIOUS LIFE

Prayer should be the key o' the day and the
lock o' the night.

In the foregoing treatment we have simply
attempted to cite and comment briefly on
some of the more outstanding events and
developments in the life of the people in
order that we might get a better perspective of the whole situation. Some
further observations on the conceptions
of the past and of the present time may
serve a useful purpose.

We have affirmed that a fair deduction
from a study of Scottish history is that
her chiefest and most distinctive characteristic lies in the realm of religion.
Religion was the prime factor in fusing
the diverse elements into a united and

47

strong people. It may have been the religion of the Old Testament, but religion nevertheless. The authority of scripture prevailed over the authority of the Church.

" It was religion that dethroned Mary and Charles I., religion that mainly influenced the policy of Charles II., and religion that cast out the Stuart dynasty in the person of James VII."

Two questions naturally arise at this point in our discussion. First, is religion subject to the same law of change governing other departments of life, such as the educational and commercial world ? and, secondly, how was religion in pre- and post-Reformation days expressed by the Church ? The answer to the first question is decidedly in the affirmative. The conditions under which people live in the twentieth century are vastly different from what they were in the first century. The conditions of life being vastly different, the mentality of the present generation cannot escape being different, hence adjustment to the new conditions is necessary. " No man putteth new wine into old wine-skins; else the wine will burst the skins, and the wine perisheth, and the skins; but they put new wine into fresh wine-skins."

To appreciate this difference we have only to pause for a moment and take some stock of the world we are now living in. Note, for example, some of the principal inventions and discoveries of the nineteenth century : railways, steam navigation, electric telegraph, the telephone, gas and electric lighting, photography, the phonograph, electrical power, Röntgen rays, anæsthetics, antiseptic surgery, and then add to these others which make their advent at a later date, like the air-flying machines, motor cars, wireless telegraphy, and television. The stupendous amount of capital invested in these modern appliances and inventions, the hundreds of thousands of men and women employed in the making, in the marketing, and in the operating of them, is of peculiar significance to those who instruct the young of our time. The thought and language of hosts of young people are, as we know, expressed in terms of their environment.

On 26th May 1923 there was issued by representative scientists, religious leaders and men of affairs, a joint statement that is apropos to the present discussion. The statement contained the following: " The purpose of science is to develop without prejudice or preconception of any kind a knowledge of the facts, the laws, and the processes of nature. The even more important task of religion, on the other hand, is to develop the consciences, the ideals, and the aspirations of mankind. Each of these two activities represents a deep and vital function of the soul of man, and both are necessary for the life, the progress, and the happiness of the human race." We will give an example of their inter-relatedness. On

The Religious Life

22nd February 1927 President Coolidge
gave an address on George Washington
in the House of Representatives. The
President spoke into a radio microphone,
and through this his voice was heard in
all parts of the country and in some of
the large cities abroad—London, Paris,
and Berlin. Literally millions of people
heard this address, extolling the private
and public character of the first President
of the United States. This is nothing
short of partnership in the cause of truth,
and these two activities can never be
divorced without weakening the structure
of human society. The same Eternal
spirit is behind all effort which seeks to
enrich and ennoble human life. Spheres
may be different, but there are values in
all of them ; the values may be different,
indeed they often are, but they are all
necessary to make up an ideal world.
This much can be said without fear of
contradiction—the spiritual is not confined to any one aspect of life. For when

we speak of the trinity of qualities, the good, the true, and the beautiful, we must admit that science as well as religion represents the true, which is as distinctly a product of the divine spirit as is the good and the beautiful. The human spirit has many ways of expressing itself. The general oversight on the part of the Church in according scanty recognition of the spiritual benefits the world has derived from art and science has tended to weaken religion.

We now come to the second question, concerning the religious conceptions held by the Church in the early period and which continued down to the time our study covers. We find it was mainly in preparing people for the next world. Most of us are familiar with the kind of hymns sung in Sunday School and Church in childhood days. It was on the happy land, far, far away, and since that was the nature of the teaching, the God invoked was also far away. He was transcendent and aloof from mundane affairs. Little was said about fitting one for the duties in the world we know something about. In these earlier days literalism and bibliolatry abounded. Individualism was particularly strong in, and outside of, the Church. It was a rare occasion when the social side of Christianity was taken as a pulpit theme. With the mind of the Church focused in preparing sinners for their mansion in the next world, what did it matter if there were thousands of houses in Scotland unfit for human habitation ?

Religion was then conceived as a finished product, " the great transaction's done." Now the purely static point of view is in the discard, and a worthier conception of life is preached. We now look at religion as adjustment, as something natural, connoting growth and service, with its roots thereof in the seen and unseen world. We hold that a timid, unadventurous religion, a religion that is conventional, balks at healthy constructive criticism, and fails to take advantage of the best and ripest knowledge and experience, can never win the respect of a growing and alert mind. This view of religion is in decided contrast to the old; the emphasis used to be placed on the depravity of man and little was said about the divinity of man. A low view of human nature is not conducive to the best results.

Science, no less than religion, is making for the growth of a world-consciousness. The people of the West are now saying to the people of the East you gave us in good measure the best religious literature there is; we give you in return our fullest measure of science, henceforth let us be loving partners in all that makes for the betterment of human kind. Because of this union, and in the interests of world-unity, we are more and more expressing our thought in universal terms. Ideas that were formerly restricted to but one aspect of life, say for instance the home, is slowly but surely extending its sphere to the entire world. After all, what makes the home delightful and precious ? It is not its finery nor furniture but the unselfish, forgiving, and generous spirit that reigns there. Then suppose we carry this same spirit into all our activities whether we be on land or sea, it is surely home for us. This is but lifting what was solely local for ages into its universal setting. Because of its larger place it ought to mean infinitely more to 'each individual and to the world at large. Big ideas like home, work, and worship can never be harnessed.

Work is devout, and service is divine,
Who stoops to scrub a floor
May worship more
Than he who kneels before a holy shrine ;
Who crushes stubborn ore
More worthily adore
Than he who crushes sacramental wine.[1]

---

[1] From " Worship " in *Odes and other Poems*, by Ronald C. Macfie.

Great ideas never perish, but they crave a change of dress occasionally. A Scottish writer expresses himself thus : " Every truth that is living will get itself said in new terms ; that is the test of its vitality, its spontaneous creative power. If we utter even our most intimate and impregnable truths in the same words twenty separate times, we will feel with dismay that we no longer believe them. A truth, like all living things, must renew its shell as well as its kernel or it shrivels and dies within the last husk which it has created for itself." [1]

The life of Scotland has suffered and does now suffer from reversing the true order of things in the religious world. It will, we think, be admitted by thoughtful students of her history that she has too often put cold theology in the forefront and pure religion in the background of her Church life. In so doing she has

[1] By Edwin Muir, in *Latitudes*.

unintentionally been untrue to the Book she most venerates—the Bible. In its final analysis it calls for a definite procedure in the life of the individual, namely, the rule and practice of the spirit of God. To say we must believe in what Calvinism stands for in order to reach this most desirable end is to contradict the common experiences of mankind. Professor William James says: "What keeps religion going is something else than abstract definitions and systems of concatenated adjectives and something different from faculties of theology and their professors."

The doctrinal sermon still retains a big place in Scottish preaching, but it is not as common as it used to be. At a dinner given to a prominent Glasgow minister last winter I was more than astonished to hear him say, in the course of his address, that he had got far enough along in life to eschew theology and politics. The fact is one could scarcely preach even the simplest kind of a sermon (certainly not in Scotland) without having one or more doctrines as a basis for one's thought. Doctrines are indispensable to the religious life, but they must be doctrines that are grounded on reason, on the deepest experiences of the past and present and in consonance with the best thought of our time. One reason why doctrinal sermons are so uninteresting is because they are so lifeless. Instead of them being the expression of something vital to life, something that one can feel and think about, they are too often but vain repetitions and high-sounding words. We need to be reminded that what fitted into the scheme of things in the sixteenth century may not fit the following, and may be a long way off from adequately serving the present.

Ideas, like eggs, become stale in the course of time. One morning at breakfast on board an Atlantic liner I ordered two soft-boiled eggs from the waiter.

The Religious Life

One of the eggs was passable, the other bordered on the stale. My messmate suggested that a little pepper would improve it. No, pepper much or little will not improve the condition of the egg, although it may make it more palatable. So with some ideas that are being constantly served to our fellow-men these days. Many of them are unwholesome, they have outlived their generation, and no amount of doctoring will improve them. There are many who are quick to detect a bad egg but are quite incapable of sensing a moribund idea.

Scotland has suffered more from being too much a slave to tradition and custom than she is conscious of; she is still, to a large extent, in the grip of a static view of life. Anyone who has been doing the same thing in the commercial, social, and religious world in precisely the same way for a given number of years when a better, " a more excellent way," is possible cannot help but suffer loss of some kind.

Her national consciousness is dimmer than it used to be. This need not be a matter of surprise to anyone conversant with the facts stated in these pages.

If her religion is to be an instrument of progress it must be like a great stream with its source in the heights, and while flowing constantly ever nourishing, purifying, and beautifying life.

(i) THE CHURCH

In the month of January (1927) the Church Advertising Department of the International Advertising Association published the results of a questionnaire conducted by 200 newspapers in sixteen cities in America. More than 125,000 persons answered the questionnaire. One of the questions asked was: "Would you be willing to have your family grow up in a community in which there is no

Church?" The reply was 13 per cent. yes and 87 per cent. no. The same question propounded in Scotland would, we think, show even a larger percentage in favour of the latter. Only a comparatively small number have any doubt as to the need of Churches in all communities. A community without a place of worship fails in one of its essentials.

Like all our institutions the Church shares in the destructive and constructive criticism of the age. Every now and then the Church is roundly denounced as almost obsolete and unworthy of support. Knowing the composition of society as we do, it is not strange that we should have periodic blasts in the moral and religious world, seeing we are accustomed to hurricanes and cyclones in the physical world. Apart, however, from all unrelated and unhistorical criticism about the Church, there are times when criticism from those outside of the Church should be patiently and conscientiously considered. There are many, like the writer, who fully appreciate what the Church has done for the intellectual and spiritual life of Scotland. One cannot forget that Scottish education from the beginning of her history is primarily religious education.

So far as we have been able to judge from expressions by those best acquainted with the work of the Church, and from our own study, there is a better feeling, a more wholesome atmosphere, among all the Churches than ever before. This is noticeable in the rallying of the different denominations around some common cause like the temperance movement, in united evangelistic work for the community, and the still larger question of Church unity, all of which indicate a perceptible widening of the Christian outlook. The people as a whole are more intelligent, more open-minded, indeed it may be said an entirely new atmosphere has been created. Dr Norman Maclean, Moderator of the

Church of Scotland, speaking at a recent meeting of the Assembly, said that when he was a young minister and came to his first few Assemblies, why, the two Assemblies breathed out threatenings—not exactly slaughter—but threatenings across the Lawnmarket year after year. It was the sort of atmosphere in which the old minister used to pray every Sunday before the General Assemblies, " Grant, Lord, that the coming Assemblies may do no harm."

Another step forward is the use of hymns and musical instruments, once barred in some churches in certain sections of the country. I distinctly remember when I was a boy it was the usual custom in our family to dole out a few sweets to each member of the family going to church on Sunday in order that we might not slumber nor sleep in the pew. This custom may not have entirely disappeared, but it is certainly not as common as formerly.

So far as the religion of the young people is concerned it is of a healthier type than was prevalent half a century ago. Then they were frequently repressed, if not suppressed; now they have in large measure won their way towards self-expression. Their religion is more natural, therefore more real.

When we come to consider the vital matter of religious education of the young, especially the kind at present in vogue in the Sunday Schools of the country, it is woefully behind the needs of the time. Neither the teaching staff, nor the subject matter provided, nor the building equipment, measures anywhere near present-day requirements, or comes near the pedagogical standard of the public school. The lesson material for the primary department, ages 5 to 8; the junior, 8 to 11; and senior, 12 and over, as published by the Scottish Sunday School Union for Christian education, and used by most of the Churches of Scotland, cannot be said to meet the moral and religious needs of those departments, nor can it give the pupil a genuine and comprehensive view of the Bible.

"We frequently hear the complaint that children, college students, or people generally do not know the Bible as well to-day as in former generations. It is doubtless true; and the Churches have themselves to blame for it. Little wonder that the Bible is a misunderstood book when one reflects upon how it has been taught. The Churches have dealt with it as a mere collection of proof-texts for their dogmas, and have failed to avail themselves of the new resources for its interpretation which the spirit of God has placed within their reach through the results of modern historical investigation.

"The Church school should be not so much a place where children may learn something or other about religion as a place where they may experience religion. It should be a fellowship of children associated in Christian living and Christian worship, under the leadership of the Church and consequently growing in Christian experiences and acquiring Christian habits, attitudes, motives, ideals, and beliefs.

" The curriculum of the Church school should therefore be pupil-centred rather than material-centred, as Sunday-school lessons have too often been. Instead of starting with a given body of material, and asking the question at what ages we may most profitably teach the different sections of this material, a truer method of curriculum-making starts with the children. It asks what are the opportunities, problems, and experiences that are normal at each stage of developing childhood; and it undertakes so to order the situations into which it brings children and the material which it makes accessible to them, as to help them meet these opportunities, solve these problems, and have these experiences." [1]

[1] From article in *Religious Education* (June 1925), by Professor Luther A. Weigle.

The Religious Life

Half a century ago comparatively little effort was made by the Church (outside of the Sunday School) to organise, discipline, inspire, and provide recreative periods for the youth of the Church. To-day nearly every Church has its Boys' Brigade and Girls' Guide organisations. The interests of the young people are in this particular a great improvement over the earlier period mentioned.

A regrettable feature of Church life is the comparatively slight appeal to the æsthetic tastes of the young people. Many of the smaller churches in Scotland, and even some of the medium-sized, resemble barns, so devoid are they of Church architecture. As for the interior, they are often inhospitable and unattractive. Most of us will admit that a refrigerator is not a place to foster worship. Principal Tulloch, in his contribution on *The Church of the Eighteenth Century*, said : " The Scottish people from the Reformation downwards had un-

happily lost the sense not only of ecclesiastical beauty but even of ecclesiastical
fitness." Since Scotland's dominant characteristic lies in the realm of religion a
larger place for the development of ecclesiastical art should be found. Human
nature will, as a rule, respond to the
best things in life. Since many of the
richest things are to be found in the
æsthetic order, all that can be done in that
realm should by all means be fostered,
for where the best things are, there God is.

So long as the Church fails to discern
the changed condition of the world, a
world which our young people have
inherited and not made, little progress
may be expected. Before we criticise
them we must look at the world in the
fifties and sixties of the last century and
what it is to-day. Everyone will admit
that it is much more complex now than
at any other period in the whole history
of Scotland. If we are willing to con-
cede that point, then we must go a step

further and admit that the education of our time does not measure up to the requirements of adolescents. The new age is not in the far distant future, it is here.

One characteristic of Church life in Scotland is worthy of mention. The life of the family and the home merges more completely into the life of the Church and the community than is noticeable in America. The bond takes the form of a goodly fellowship ; young and old of both sexes feel and share the joys and sorrows common to humanity. The feeling is akin to that expressed by Betty when addressing Maister Weelum in *Betty Grier*. " But, oh, my boy ! in ocht that may in the future distress ye dinna leave Betty oot, an' dinna forget that her he'rt is big eneuch to haud your sorrows as weel as her ain." [1]

In an age predominantly scientific, an age when the attractions to all classes

[1] By J. L. Waugh, p. 42.

were never more numerous and seductive, the Church still remains in Scotland a mighty bulwark and power. This is said in the full awareness of the fact that many churches have meagre congregations. Part of this difficult situation grows out of a lack of adjustment to the actual requirements of our age, and the adherence to medieval conceptions, and the use of a phraseology that is outworn. Most of the Scripture texts used as the basis for pulpit themes in the Scottish pulpit to-day are used haphazardly, used regardless of the particular passages being good or bad psychology. It is too often taken for granted that because it is taken from the Bible it must be all right. Little regard is paid to the principle of selection. For example, most of us know that the heart " is deceitful above all things " and " exceedingly corrupt," but is it a wise or gracious thing to be constantly reminding a patient who is extremely weak that he is " desperately " sick ?

Is there not another and better aspect of man's nature to which we can make an appeal? We all know there is, such as radiating cheer, giving encouragement and hope, inspiring men so that the latent and potential qualities may be quickened and brought into everyday use. It is in this direction that we add to the moral and intellectual capital of the world. But more than that must be noted to account for the apathy towards the Church and the decline in Church attendance.

In recent years the press has become a great and growing factor in the life of the community. The best of the newspapers in Scotland, as in America, are never dull—they cannot afford to be. They throb with news of keen interest to the reader; they carry considerable informative and cultural material. It is no wonder that many find the newspapers more interesting than many Church services. What the Church has lost in numbers and influence has to some extent been taken over by the press. That part of it which is governed by a high moral standard has become an instrument for good in the land, and is bound to play a still greater role in weakening Church-going. The press has the advantage of the Church in bringing before its readers the great local, national, and world happenings, all the marvellous changes that have and are taking place. The Church often forgets that we are living in a totally different world from the world in which our fathers and mothers lived, but that part of the press we have in mind never does.

A single illustration at this point may suffice to suggest the nature of the world in which we are living. The comparatively recent history-making flight to Australia by Sir Alan Cobham, travelling 28,000 miles to Australia and back, occupied only thirteen flying days. Referring to this marvellous feat the present

The Religious Life

Prime Minister of Australia said that when his father and mother went to Australia sixty or seventy years ago it took them over six months. The press gave unusual space to Cobham's accomplishment, and everybody admired the skill and courage of the aviator. Such feats as these are clear intimations of greater things to come. Meanwhile, we can see that they give the promise of annihilating distance, of bringing the people of the world closer, all of which tends clearly in the direction of spiritual unity. The spiritual quality is never absent from a great achievement. Religion and science are both engaged in a mighty crusade for the betterment of the world. In spirit they are one and inseparable.

The population of Scotland is less than five millions. Out of that small population it is calculated that in 1921 there were 1,067,656 non-Church-going adults above twenty years of age, and there are now approximately 1,107,000 non-Church-going adults, of whom the vast majority are Protestant. It is also calculated that there are at least 141,000 Protestant children, between the ages of five and fourteen, who do not attend any Sunday School, and that there are 267,000 Protestant adolescents who do not attend any Bible Class. This indifference to one of our great institutions is not confined to any one country. According to the report of the Continuation Committee to the Interchurch Conference, held in Philadelphia, Pa., U.S.A., a short time ago, it appears that " in thirteen communions with a grand total of 15,160,170 members, the losses aggregate 268,065. As the total of evangelical membership is upwards of 29,000,000, the total yearly loss, if other communions beside the thirteen were included, would approximate 500,000."

Disquieting as these figures are, it is but one aspect of an even larger question connected with Church life. Is it not true that many of those who attend the regular services of the Church do so because there is no alternative before them ; because it has been and is now the custom of the family to attend Church ; because it is the respectable thing to do ? To put the case in another way, for many there would seem to be no deep interest in the services ; no real longing for the house of worship ; no feeling that soul hunger will be satisfied. This is not speculative reasoning but actual fact. To what extent it is true it would be difficult to say.

Dismal as the foregoing may appear, there is an extremely hopeful side to this difficult question. It was said of Calvin that the religious instinct was the master-principle of his life. With equal force it may be said to be the master-principle of nearly every Scotsman whether in or out of the Church. Herein, then, lies not stony but good ground in which to sow the seed that will in due time bring forth an abundant harvest.

A prominent preacher from Scotland visited America a few years ago. It was at a time when the press were discussing the reasons why working-men do not go to Church. This preacher was asked to contribute to a magazine symposium his views on the subject. To the one who solicited his expression the reply was : " If they want to hear me let them come to Church." This is neither New Testament teaching nor the way to build up a congregation.

In these pages we have stressed the idea that what a community or country can do best is the steadfast thing to do. To carry this thought out to its logical conclusion means that quality must be the chief aim of whatever is undertaken. When men are insufficiently prepared for a particular vocation, the work about to be undertaken must necessarily suffer. It is the absence of fitness and the inability to sense the needs of the age that is responsible for most of the unedifying work of the Church. A skilled workman is always appreciated and is seldom jobless.

(ii) THE FIRST DAY OF THE WEEK

Those born in Scotland half a century ago need scarcely be reminded of the way Sunday was observed. On that day we wore our nattiest clothes. Even that was something to look forward to, for the change in attire had a good psychological effect. We were not allowed to travel on any kind of conveyance to church or any other place. As for the reading of fiction it was considered an almost heinous offence. Only literature of the so-called pious type was permitted.

In a review of a new book entitled *Donald Macleod of Glasgow* in the *Scotsman* of 28th February 1927, the following is pertinent here : " The reader of to-day would probably be highly amused at some of the changes which Macleod [he was a brother of Norman Macleod], out of regard for the crochets of subscribers, was led to make in MSS. which he accepted for publication. In *The Trumpet Major* of Mr Thomas Hardy, which appeared in *Good Words* in 1880, Sunday, the day of the week for which two lovers have arranged a meeting, is altered to Monday. As the appointed day draws near, and during its course, allusions such as ' that Sabbath day,' ' it being Sunday,' as well as references to Church and Prayer-book, are removed, and there are found to be necessary changes of a more serious nature, which, as made by the editor, move one to admiration of his ingenuity." To-day it would move one to a denunciation of his easy compliance.

We often wonder why the present generation are not better than they are. The wonder is that they are not worse. Over-strictness, repression, and a failure to understand the young, growing mind may produce temporary results pleasing

The Religious Life

to adults, but a reaction is inevitable. The observance of the Sunday in the sixties and seventies of the last century was far too much touched by severity and gloom instead of serenity and gladness.

The growth of knowledge and the coming of a larger spirit into civilisation has produced a change for the better. The old rigidity and puritanical elements have for the most part disappeared. Yet when all that is admitted I am not at all convinced that all is well concerning The First Day of the Week. We cannot shut our eyes to facts. There is the steady decline in Church attendance ; there is a growing multitude of pleasure-seekers on Sunday, and the number of people who are just apathetic concerning the claims of " The First Day of the Week " are multiplying.

The younger generation have evidently not got a grip of the real value of this day. It is not simply a question of the promulgation of a law on Sabbath-keeping from Mount Sinai or a reaffirmation of the principle in early Christian thought which we have to keep in mind. The whole matter harks back to the very nature of man in his primeval state. In the course of time the discovery was made that man's estate demanded a day set apart from other days wherein man could rest from his toil. The need of this day became so obvious that the older civilisations have simply passed the tradition to present-day life because it voiced what was true to the nature of man's constitution and therefore necessary for his well-being.

When the question of Sunday golf came up for consideration before the Town Council of St Andrews, several men known to the community were invited to express their views on the subject. Among them was the well-known golfer Tom Morris. When asked for his opinion he modestly said, " The ground is used six days in the week, *gie* it a rest on Sunday."

80

The Religious Life

We have entitled this chapter "The First Day of the Week" advisedly. We believe the evidence for its quiet, meditative observance is overwhelming. It is not only first, numerically speaking, of all the days of the week, but first spiritually. In the restfulness of that day a season of helpful meditation may be opened up to one, or a new vision and a more appreciative sense of the unseen experienced. The visible world is not all of life by a long way. Perhaps much of our soul impoverishment and our inability to meet the problems here is due to a too restricted world and an indifference to the larger spiritual universe —the invisible.

(iii) The Bible

The following advertisement appeared on the first page of *The Glasgow Herald* for 27th September 1926 :

Scotland through American Eyes

" SCOTLAND in 1856 was a BIBLE-LOVING, SAB-
BATH-KEEPING LAND, in 1926 is a BIBLE-
NEGLECTING, SABBATH-BREAKING LAND.

' It is appointed unto men once to die, but
after this the judgment.'—Hebrews ix. 27.

' We must all appear before the judgment seat
of Christ that every one may receive the things
done in his body—whether it be good or bad.'—
2 Corinthians v. 10.

' Behold I come quickly : and my reward is
with me, to give every man according as his
work shall be.'—Revelation xxii. 12.

' Repent ye therefore and be converted, that
your sins may be blotted out.'—Acts iii. 19.

' Go ye into all the world, and preach the
Gospel to every creature.'—St Mark xvi. 15.

' Pray ye therefore the Lord of the harvest,
that He will send forth labourers into His
harvest.'—St Matthew ix. 38.

' Ye also helping together by prayer.'—
2 Corinthians i. 11."

If the statement preceding the Scripture references and the passages quoted
are intended to influence people concerning the better observance of the Sabbath,

or to bring conviction on some moral or religious duty, they are doomed to failure. For no intelligent person can ever be convinced or edified by distorting Bible teaching. To wrest the Scriptures to suit one's preconceptions is a common and mischievous practice. The conclusion to be drawn from this advertising propaganda is that those who do not keep the Sabbath as they were accustomed to do in 1856 are Sabbath-breakers. Scotland, we are told, was Bible-loving in 1856 and Bible-neglecting in 1926. If those directing this propaganda were asked the simple question, Which year would you prefer to live in, 1856 or 1926 ? does anyone doubt what the answer would be ?

The misuse of the Bible is a common practice in our day. We will furnish two examples out of a score or more which might be cited—one out of the Old, and the other from the New Testament.

Scotland through American Eyes

I attended a union Christmas Service
in Washington, D.C., in December 1925,
at which the President and his family
attended. The order of exercises were
printed on a four-page folder and the
responsive reading was taken from Is.
xi. 1–9 ; ix. 6–7. The reason for this
particular selection was in keeping with
the old traditional view that it refers
to Christ, who was to come about eight
centuries after the time these words were
spoken. A careful reading of the book
will show that the writer did not have
the Christ of the gospels in mind, but
one who was to come soon. It is
true that in some respects Christ fulfilled
the words found in these chapters, but it
is now generally agreed among modern
scholars that it has no direct bearing on
Jesus of Nazareth. In this same order
of exercises the Authorised Version of the
Bible was used ; note what it says :
Is. xi. 3 reads : " . . . and he shall not
judge after the sight of his eyes, neither

reprove after the hearing of his ears; but with righteousness shall he judge the poor and reprove with equity for the meek of the earth." In the American Standard Version the word used for "reprove" is "decide." That makes sense; the other does not convey the meaning the author had in mind.

From the gospels and Paul's epistles the teaching is clear that the early Christians believed in the speedy and physical return of Jesus from heaven. There has been, as we know, no return in that sense; still, we have a great body of sincere and devout people who still cherish and hold on to the belief of those early Christians. One would almost conclude from such hideboundness that the spirit of God had ceased to operate and that no new knowledge and facts had come into the world since the first century. A corrective for this static, antiquated, and traditional use of the Bible is to be found in a right approach to the Old and New Testament and adopting modern methods of study. People have nothing to fear from constructive criticism of the Bible. What they have to dread most of all is the form of theological and religious Bolshevism that poisons the mind of young people, and does injustice to the fairest and finest religious literature in the world.

One would imagine that in religious Scotland most of the Protestant population knew the names of the different books of the Bible. But such is not the case. A minister in a city of over 50,000 inhabitants in announcing the reading of the morning lesson from the book of Haggai took occasion to inform the congregation where it was located. Yet it would be found that many of those in that particular congregation were never at a loss to buttress their political and religious opinions by Bible quotations. As for knowing the Bible comprehensively, historically, and religiously the people of Scotland have a great and glorious task awaiting them.

It is particularly unfortunate that so many are either unaware, or are apathetic or hostile towards one of the significant movements of our time—historical criticism. This movement has brought light and deliverance to many seekers after Bible truth, and has paved the way for the reshaping and rebuilding of doctrine.

THE INDUSTRIAL LIFE

CHAPTER III

THE INDUSTRIAL LIFE

Difficulties are whetstones to exertion.

FOR the larger part of the nineteenth century Great Britain was generally regarded as the workshop of the world. It was not until the closing years of that century that new forces entered the industrial arena and keen international rivalry began. It is seldom that all the economic and commercial advantages lie in one direction or with one country. One country may have more of the great natural resources, such as coal and iron, than another; or it may be that the particular fiscal policies of the great industrial countries may be different; or that technical education may be further advanced in one or two, over the others;

or, finally, in the ability of some countries making adjustment to new conditions more rapidly than others. These are all factors in the rise and fall in the industrial world. It may be too much to expect of any one nation first to achieve leadership in industry and then to hold it.

It is the testimony of W. L. MacKenzie King, Prime Minister of Canada; Stanley Melbourne Bruce, Prime Minister of Australia; and Joseph Gordon Coates, Prime Minister of New Zealand; and some others that might be mentioned, that the Scots have been pioneers in the national life, not only of the countries mentioned, but in many other parts of the world. As world-builders they have filled a high and honourable place. Yet, when we come to examine industrial affairs in the homeland during the last generation and more, pioneering is not there, at least to the same extent. Take the matter of the motor revolution for example. Henry Ford, in his book *To-day and To-morrow*, says : " On October last, 1908, we made the first of our present type of small cars ; on June 4th, 1924, we made the ten millionth ; now, in 1926, we are on our thirteenth million." Nearly every Britisher knows that it was many years after the first mentioned date when motor cars of a similar type were built in this country.

The *London Times* of 9th November 1926 says : " In the matter of the provision of a cheap and easily available supply of electric power this country has admittedly been outdistanced by its commercial rivals among the nations of the world."

In the discussion of the Electricity Bill in the House of Lords in November 1926, the Earl of Balfour said :

If we had reformed our system, as we might have done, many years ago, an immense amount of public money would have been saved, as again an immense amount of money would be saved by dealing with the problem now instead of leaving it to the future.

Scotland through American Eyes

In opening an exhibition in the Science Museum, South Kensington, London, a short time ago, the following timely words were spoken by the same statesman :

It is not sufficiently realised that if we are to be a great progressive nation it can be only by the application of science and a basic knowledge of the laws of nature upon which more and more we perceive the future of mankind is going to depend. I should like to say to every party in industrial controversy that if the general level or standard of life is to be maintained and improved it can only be by the more and more successful application of increasing knowledge to the production of wealth upon which the whole community is predestined to share.

At the Annual Dinner of the Scottish Centre of the Institution of Electrical Engineers, held last winter in Glasgow, the Secretary of State for Scotland said : " Compared with other great peoples, in spite of all our learning and progress, we were far behind in the development of electrical power." A leader entitled

The Industrial Life

" Lessons from America " in *The Scotsman* of 5th August 1927, says : " Since 1850, when Britain's economic supremacy was unchallenged and seemed unchallenge-able, when we produced two-thirds of the world's coal, two-thirds of the world's iron and steel, two-thirds of the world's cotton goods, and owned two-thirds of the world's shipping, our place in the world has altered, somewhat for the worse."

These brief references might be multi-plied, but we think they are sufficient to indicate the precise point where Scotland, like England, has failed. It is clearly in the lack of the application of science to the practical life of the last thirty or forty years. A country cannot fall behind in the industrial race (especially an in-dustrial centre like the Clyde Valley), without affecting her economic, social, and moral status.

It is gratifying to note that a great electrical power scheme is now in process of development in Scotland. The scheme will affect a population of over 3,761,200, and an area (largely industrial) of about 5000 square miles.

It is only within the last few years that Britain began to send over to the United States of America delegations to study industrial conditions there. Had this been part of the programme long before trade began to languish, before her industrial supremacy was challenged and contested, she certainly would have been in a much better condition to meet the open competition in the markets of the world.

In the report of the delegation appointed by the Minister of Labour to study industrial conditions in Canada and the United States of America, with special reference to the relations between employers and employees in their bearing upon industrial conditions in Great Britain, the delegates visited sixteen cities in Canada and fifty in the U.S. The first thing mentioned in the report is that " each industrial country has difficulties, as well as opportunities for advancement, peculiar to itself, and no one will assume that methods which are practicable in one country are necessarily suited to another." Then this report goes on to say :

Experiments that are being made in Canada, the United States, and other industrial countries can teach valuable lessons in the solution of problems which are common to all phases of industry, and in our view the frequent interchange of visits by representatives of both management and labour is to be encouraged. Such visits lead to a wider outlook and give encouragement in the continued application to our own problems.

The main points in this report refer to the value of industrial combination, intelligent standardisation, simplification of design so that parts of any commodity can be more cheaply and easily manufactured, instalment buying, the recognition of management, the attitude of labour and industrial relations.

Any scheme which does not provide for conditions which will raise the moral and economic standard of the men employed is sure to fail. Industry can only be peaceful when the spirit of co-operation between management and employees has full play. The report referred to says :

There is no doubt that where an opportunity for representation and self-expression has been given to the workpeople it has reduced strife and made for harmonious and prompt settlements of grievances, while providing opportunity for discussing in a business-like way the problems that arise between the management and employees. The schemes have been successful where management and labour have acted in good faith, and each has shown confidence in the other. They have failed where there has been absence of good faith and confidence.

An intelligent thesis of existence calls for a close study of the hunger and love instincts. It is here where much of the chaos in our social system originates. We have too often disassociated what should be associated. We have ignorantly and wilfully divorced healthy instincts, like hunger and love, which were intended to operate harmoniously. One we have characterised as lying in the field of economics and the other as in the region of the spiritual, when in reality they are both vitally related, and when rightly viewed and used, both are spiritual.

What is Scotland's main problem ? It is the problem of the four continents, and the islands of the sea, " the jar of meal and the cruse of oil," or if one wants to give it a school name, it is the economic problem. It enters nearly every door in every land. At a Presbytery meeting in the northern part of Scotland in the month of June 1927 a minister said :

. . . We are not getting nowadays the number of students sufficient to fill our pulpits, nor are we getting the quality of students we were accustomed to in the past. The principal reason to account for this was the inadequacy of the emoluments provided for the ministry of the Church of Scotland, and then it was considered that other professions were offering inducements to young men far in excess of what the Church could offer. The young men of to-day were more or less justified in the attitude they were taking up. His own judgment was that poverty was the common lot of a great majority of the clergy of the Church of Scotland at the present time. . . .

This is a lamentable situation. It presents a distinct challenge to the manhood and womanhood of Scotland to meet this matter squarely and promptly. It is another illustration of what we have affirmed in these pages that the controlling factor in human life in all civilised countries lies in the economic realm.

In a recent article Bertrand Russell said, " The fundamental delusion of our time, in my opinion, is the excessive emphasis upon the economic aspects of life, and I do not expect the strife between capitalism and communism as philosophies to cease until it is recognised

100

that both are inadequate through their failure to recognise biological needs." [1] The " excessive emphasis " is now being partly met by a movement for the humanisation of industry. It looks as though we were on the threshold of a new era in industry, when a multi-millionaire and a large employer of labour in America can declare " the working man should be made to feel that he was as important as a capitalist " (Dec. 17, 1927).

The strenuous effort now being made in Britain to foster Empire products and to induce the people of the British Isles to purchase them may have a temporary but not ultimate success. People who are intelligent will in the last analysis purchase the goods or articles that suit them as to price and quality, whether they are made or grown within or outside the Empire. What is more to the point, is to produce things that are not

[1] *The Century Magazine*, January 1928.

only as good as what other countries produce, but something a shade better. What Scotland can do better than other countries, that thing Scotland should do. When that policy is pursued there will be no difficulty in finding a market for the country's products. We develop and become strong by making the fullest use of our powers and opportunities.

The following extract from a recent article by V. M. Kipp, dated Ottawa, December 9th, 1927, and published in the *New York Times* two days later, confirms the position taken in these pages :

" Those who hold to the theory that trade follows the flag have something to think about in Canadian statistics for the twelve months to October 31. In that period Canada's trade with the United States amounted to the huge total of $1,180,000,000, which—and this is an important point—was $437,000,000 greater than the entire trade with the British Empire.

"We exported to the United States goods worth $472,000,000 and imported to the value of $707,000,000, leaving an unfavourable balance of $235,000,000. To Great Britain and British Dominions and colonies, on the other hand, we sent goods valued at $511,000,000, while from them we imported to the extent of only $231,000,000, creating a balance in Canada's favour of $280,000,000.

"For the most part Canadians refuse to show alarm over the condition of affairs. They buy the goods which please them, and patriotic preference has little to do with the selection of markets. Other things being equal, the average Canadian will buy a British-made product in preference to an article from another country, but he does not propose to suffer the slightest personal inconvenience in order that inter-empire trade may be developed.

"An English automobile is a rarity on the street of any Canadian city. Canadian drug stores are stocked with

American goods ; much of the ready-to-
wear clothing comes from the United
States, little of it from Great Britain.
American periodicals, in particular the
popular weeklies, circulate in Canada in
immense numbers, and so we are sus-
ceptible to precisely the same influences
which sell bath tubs, silk stockings, and
radio receivers to the great American
public."

When the new Ford car was introduced
in New York city on December 2nd,
1927, the above newspaper mentioned in
its news column the name of the first
purchaser, and then added that another
early buyer was a bishop (the name was
given) from Aberdeen, Scotland.

When Elihu Root was Secretary of
State—appointed to the office in 1905—
he visited some of the South American
republics. On his return he addressed
a body of business men—I think it was
in New York city. One remark he made
at that time has always remained with

104

me. It was to this effect—when the manufacturers of the United States make what the people of the South American republics want, they will get their trade. The best comment on that policy is to quote a few figures. I find the exports to Latin America in 1922 were 536 million dollars, three years later 845 million, and in 1926, 879 million. The percentage of increase in 1926 over the years 1910–1914 was 191 per cent., and over the year 1922, 64 per cent. The years mentioned ended June 30th.

In an article on Anglo-Brazilian trade in *The London Times* for June 21st, 1927, the Secretary of the British Chamber of Commerce, San Paulo, said, "In general terms the loss of trade [British] may be attributed to the employment by competitors of more up-to-date and modern trading methods." We see, therefore, that ability plus adaptability are essential to any country seeking wider markets.

Since industrial occupations offer one

of the best ways whereby the mind and the body can be used to promote health and wealth, a few words in commendation of a larger place for rural industries in Scotland may be said.

Machinery is a big and important factor in industry to-day. It has almost revolutionised the entire world. This is not only evident in the incalculable output of things, but in cheapening what we eat and wear, and in marketing many labour-saving devices. Much can be said in favour of modern machinery, yet it must be acknowledged that it has tended to depersonalise men and women. In other words, the human element is lacking. In rural industries there is a distinct place for the strengthening of character. Skill, initiative, and excellence are all required, qualities which as a rule are absent from those who do mere machine work. Handmade articles of the right kind will always find a market, and nowhere more than in the United States of America.

THE TRUE CONCEPTION
OF WORK

CHAPTER IV

THE TRUE CONCEPTION OF WORK

Who works for justice, works with Thee,
Who works in love, Thy child shall be.
                    SAMUEL LONGFELLOW

FEW people are aware of the danger arising from a life wherein ease, apathy, and unemployment is coveted. Natures so afflicted become in time the breeding-places for individual ailments and social discontent. At best it is only a matter of a few years when such persons are overtaken by a biological law which eliminates them. This law, unlike some of our laws on the statute books, is inescapable. In the light of this stern fact no greater harm has befallen this land than the inability of the community to deal effectively with the momentous question of unemployed men and women. This we think will become more apparent as we try to present the positive side of this theme.

Employment means infinitely more than wages. To be engaged in some steady occupation calls for the exercise of one's faculties and powers. It is in the use of these that we attain health, happiness, and growth. Without self-activity there is no possible way of reaching what is beautiful, what is good, and what is true in life. The kingly men and queenly women are those who make full use of all their powers, their faculties, and their gifts for the highest ends.

Most of the work done in the world to-day may be said to be done out of sheer necessity. Families have to be provided for in many different ways, rents have to be met, provision made for sickness, and so on. The compulsory element in work has much in its favour, but the whole conception of work should be placed where it rightly belongs, on a much higher level. When we consider the large number of men and women unemployed, and those who play the game of "ca' canny," and the men who have a keen distaste for work of any kind, it cannot very well be said that society is in a healthy state. "In an inquiry which was made in Britain, out of nearly 5000 workers only about 13 per cent. declared themselves to be interested in their trade, and the percentage varied with the different trades." [1]

When we look at this whole question of the output of one's energies practically and thoughtfully what does it yield? Take, for example, the case of a man engaged in making or in helping to make some useful article. In doing his particular part he is giving, we will say, the best of his mental and physical powers, and when this work is done consciously

[1] Professor E. P. Cathcart in an Address at Glasgow University.

and well, he is actually rendering a spiritual service. San Bernardino of Siena, who by the way was a follower of St Francis, certainly caught the spirit of that profound utterance in the New Testament, " My father worketh even until now and I work." Note well his brief homily : " I want this morning to teach you how to pray. If you spin with a good heart, do you know that you pray with effect ? Here is a piece of news for you ! While you work you can pray and not even be aware of it. And you who do your trade well and honestly, all the time you work, you pray. Do you make shoes ? Do you make wool ? Are you a carpenter or a mason ? Are you a smith, or what is it you do ? Whatever it is, if you do it well, you are praying all the time."

What a fine vision of reality. San Bernardino saw the ordinary, but very necessary, work of life done by the everyday man as prayer. He discerned in

The True Conception of Work

all this kind of work a genuine outflow
of spiritual energy, and this indeed is
religion.

The Romans dignified and glorified
work. Some of their maxims are familiar
to us. "Labour is pleasure itself,"
"Labour conquers all things," "To work
is to pray."

Would anyone say that the Master of
Men in mending and making tables and
chairs was not doing spiritual work?
What makes the work spiritual? We
answer, when it is done with a high purpose in mind, done consciously, honestly,
and well.

The real prayers of the people are
in the workshop, factories, offices, every
place where men are performing their
private or public duties. It is there
where all that constitutes mind and body
are freely given for others, and it is in
this giving that we find our true selves.
It is there where the real altars are, and
the sacrificial element most in evidence.

All honourable work is the outpouring and offering of one's highest self; it is genuine prayer and the fulfilment of spiritual law. There is no better place in all the world for the deepening of the spiritual life than where one is, and in doing well whatever work one may be called upon to do.

The sad thing is that employers and employees have, as a rule, never connected life in the commercial and industrial world with the redemption of man. Stale theology looks at a man as vile, and a considerable part of the employers in the business and industrial world regard their employees as mere money-makers for them. Not until we can get a new vision of man's worth, and are able to see first of all the divine in him and in all forms of useful and uplifting activity, will it be possible to get the world's work performed on a humaner and higher level.

THE EDUCATIONAL LIFE

CHAPTER V

THE EDUCATIONAL LIFE

The price of wisdom is above rubies.

PEOPLE who exclaim " O that it were
as it hath been " seldom know how rich
we are to-day, compared with former
times, in all that goes into the making
of our lives.

At one period in the history of Scotland education was largely in the hands
of the Church. There was a school,
one might say, in connection with every
parish; now it is in other hands, the
State. From the time of the Reformation to the passing of the Act of 1872
" the appointment of the masters of the
parish schools was entirely in the hands
of the Church of Scotland . . . the school
boards were brought into existence by

this act." There were good and sufficient reasons for this change. The field
of intellectual activity was widening;
industry was making tremendous strides;
new interests were coming to the front
and demanding attention, all of which
called for adjustment and adaptation in
the educational world. The State could
meet this new condition more readily
and more effectively than the Church.
Time has justified the change, for to-day
it may be fairly claimed that in the
main the schools of Scotland have kept
pace with modern educational methods
and theories.

But this qualifying sentence leaves
something to be desired. We have maintained throughout these pages that times
have changed, and are changing, hence
we need the kind of education that will
amply meet the new situation. A fine
example of how modern thought views
things is given by Professor Wm. H.
Kilpatrick of Columbia University, New

York, in his admirable little book on *Education for a Changing Civilisation.* He says, " Modern thought increasingly bases itself upon internal authority. Historic religious progress has moved successively from the extreme of external authority, that of the Church, through a combination of external and internal authority, that of the private interpretation of the Bible, to a position frankly internal as to authority, accepting that as religiously true which most deeply meets one's felt religious needs." The problem then would be to assist young people " to make the shift from external authority to internal authority." Further on he says, " Our duty is so to prepare the rising generation to think that they can and will think for themselves, even ultimately, if they so decide, to the point of revising or rejecting what we now think. Our chosen beliefs will have to stand this ordeal."

One is impressed with the seriousness

and thoroughness of the work undertaken and accomplished. The old educational system differs from the new in that the former put the stress on the intellectual side, whereas the new aims at developing almost every side of the pupils' nature.

In looking over the Annual Report of the Education Authority of Glasgow for the session of 1925–26 one is astounded at the amount of thought and provision made for the child of to-day. The total number of pupils for whom the Education Authority of Glasgow alone is responsible borders closely on 190,000. By means of their remarkable medical service they are able to ascertain the condition of every school child, "and deal with every case where the cause is neglect or lack of food and clothing."

Medical treatment is provided free of charge for all children whose parents, in the view of the Authority, are not financially able to provide adequate private treatment, and in all cases the Authority take steps to secure that immediate treatment is given, and that the treatment is regular and continuous until the desired effect has been obtained. . . .

Almost every conceivable defect in the child's physical and mental side is attended to, and what is so thoroughly done for the defective and abnormal child has its counterpart in the numerous and special activities in art, science, and religion arranged so as to meet the needs of the ordinary pupil.

While the " objects of the Authority are primarily preventive rather than merely ameliorative," and while it is of the greatest importance to put the health of the child in the forefront, one wonders, after reading this report, whether the education based on attempting to do so much for the pupil is, after all, the best thing for his development. Does it bring out the best that is in the pupil ? Does it minister to the self-realisation of the individual ? On the whole, we do not think it does, as the tendency among hosts of young people, as well as people who are no longer young, is to do as little as possible, certainly no more than they have to do.

One of the tendencies in Britain is to look to the State for assistance in too many directions. So long as this tendency prevails the advancement of the individual is retarded and endangered. " It is significant to remember," says an editorial in *The Scotsman* for 5th August 1927, " that Britain's prosperity was won and retained at a time when individualism and leadership were left unfettered, and has been lost largely through the handicapping of these qualities." On the other hand, if the young were taught at an early age the importance of self-culture and self-government and what they owe to society, namely, certain duties and responsibilities, it would make the question of their rights a simpler problem. As the years roll along our problems do not seem to lessen, which is equivalent to saying our ability to think correctly is inadequate.

In the last analysis all public questions are in reality educational ones. Let us suppose that all those in Scotland who are at present unemployed, and all those who have experienced a long time of unemployment in the past, had been given some practical lessons on sociology, would any condition such as is described in the following quotation ever have taken place : " During the past few years hundreds of millions of pounds have been paid out either through the employment exchanges or the Poor Law authorities and not a stroke of work has been done in return." [From *The Evening Citizen*, Glasgow, 18th June 1927.]

Every thinking person will admit that there is nothing that tends so much to individual deterioration and national insolvency than doling out money without getting an adequate return in the shape of work.

There is another situation which we believe most Scotsmen would say demands attention. At the Annual Meeting of the Scottish Children's League of Pity (3rd June 1927) the Duke of Montrose said : "Did it not strike them as a very sad thing that in this country, supposed to be the most civilised nation of the world and the centre of Christianity . . . they had 21,000 children in a position of neglect and pity. . . . It was all very well for public authorities to provide the means of looking after the children when they were in distress and trouble, but wouldn't it be better to try and get the parents so educated that they themselves looked after the children, instead of the public authorities." This would seem to be a herculean task, but the last thing an educator should admit is saying, "It can't be done !" Anything that will diminish the spirit of paternalism is to be commended.

Let us not forget that many of Scotland's most illustrious sons reached exalted heights without any assistance from the State. Think of Burns's scanty intellectual fare compared with what is now available in the public libraries and schools of this land. The books most commonly used in the school of his time were the Bible, Mason's *Collection of Prose and Verse*, and Fisher's *English Grammar*. " The first two books I ever read in private and which gave me more pleasure than any two books I ever read," he said, " were *The Life of Hannibal* and the *History of Sir William Wallace*." Now, this is what we are interested in bringing before the youth of this land at this particular point. His poems and songs are now translated into very many of the languages in the world, and to-day there are in the Scottish Poets' Corner in The Mitchell Library, Glasgow, between 6000 and 7000 volumes (in at least 600 different editions) of the poet's writings and also several hundred books about the author and his productions. What aid did the national bard get from the State ?

No help, nor hope, nor view had I, nor person
    to befriend me ;
So I must toil, and sweat, and moil, and labour
    to sustain me ;
To plough and sow, to reap and mow, my
    father bred me early ;
For one, he said, to labour bred, was a match
    for Fortune fairly.

We shall admire Burns all the more when we grasp the full significance for our time of the ballad entitled " My Father was a Farmer," from which the above lines are taken. In these days, when so much time and energy are consumed in artificial exercises, we need to be reminded that the best kind of physical education must be based on racial evolution. The race has come to its present stage mainly through industrial activities, and these we cannot forego without serious loss. Burns said that the great misfortune of his life was to lack an aim. A curriculum that would aim at developing an all-round personality, a sense of social obligations, and give a large place to the creative side of the pupil's life, would be working in the direction of a specific aim.

Modern views of education are alive to the achievements of mankind. Recently a French writer, Raymond Gérard, seized the opportunity to write an article in *L'Echo des Sports*, extolling Captain Lindbergh's education. Lindbergh, it will be remembered, made a non-stop flight between New York and Paris, a distance of 3610 miles, in about $33\frac{1}{2}$ hours. We quote:

The marvellous exploit achieved by Charles Lindbergh was due to exceptional qualities of courage and cool judgment. But one can say also that it is a product of the advantages of American education. Lindbergh, in physique and in morale, is a representative type of the younger generation of Americans.

There is a world of difference between the shaping of minds in France and the preparation for life in America. French education is an affair of classes, of lessons, of studies, during which we pitchfork into the mind of the student the innumerable matters of school curriculums. The brain of a French high-school pupil is like a steamer trunk into which one packs a lot of widely different articles without regard to the destination of the tourist.

American education is not at all like that. Before setting a big pile of books before the pupil, the teacher asks himself: "Where are we going? What is the ideal to be attained?" The Greeks sought happiness through beauty. Modern nations seek to dominate by force. All right! Force is not obtained through books. For one sage we have ten men of action. Science can help, but the source of energy lies in character.

Lindbergh, the big blond boy with blue eyes, is the product of an education that teaches how to apply all the known sciences, how to be inventive, ingenious, able to solve enigmas.

We have seen nothing briefer and better in the essentials of education than the little book by Dr Thomas J. Jones on *Four Essentials of Education*. The preface is written by Professor F. H. Giddings of Columbia University, New York, in which he says that the "essentials of education for the masses of mankind comprise more than the three R's. Four basic ones are : (1) knowledge and mastery of hygiene and health ; (2) knowledge and mastery of the resources and opportunities, in particular the agricultural and climatic ones, of the local physical environment from which a community must obtain its livelihood ; (3) knowledge and mastery of a decent and comfortable life, without degradation of women and children on which race advancement and vitality depend ; and (4) knowledge and mastery of the art of recreation in a broad meaning of the word, the art of creating a sane and elastic personality, self-controlled and poised, serene of mind and capable of happiness."

· · · · ·

Health.—Thirty-eight years after Allan Ramsay was born (1686) he wrote a poem entitled " Health," two lines of which ran thus :

Luxurious Man ! Although thou'rt blessed with
    wealth,
    Why should thou use it to destroy thy health ?

Seventy-three years after the birth of
the author of the " Gentle Shepherd "
there was born, in a shire almost adjoining
the one where Ramsay first saw the light
of day, the revered Robert Burns. The
following four lines from his poem " My
Father was a Farmer," and the above
two lines from Ramsay should ever be
remembered :

All you who follow wealth and power
    With unremitting ardour, O,
The more in this you look for bliss,
    You leave your view the farther, O.

Professor William James says : " There
is not a single one of our states of mind,
high or low, healthy or morbid, that has
not some organic process as its condition."
In the light of this statement it is gratifying to know that the hygienic conditions
in Scotland are vastly better than they
were fifty years ago. It is fully recog-

nised by the Health Authorities in Scotland, " That physical inefficiency was at once the most permanent and fruitful cause of individual unhappiness and social discontent." Physical inefficiency means of course lessened production, and this in turn makes it more difficult for a country to compete successfully with other countries.

The eighth annual report (1926) of the Scottish Board of Health states that the general death-rate in 1926 was 13·0 per 1000 persons living. This is the lowest recorded in Scotland except in the year 1923, when it was 12·9.

There is also an encouraging statement in this report concerning housing conditions in Scotland since the War. From 1919 until the end of 1926, under all the State-aided schemes, 49,808 houses had been built and other 28,450 were under construction or approved. " Over 10,000 houses in slum-clearing schemes are being closed, and 9596 new or reconstructed houses are being built to replace them."

This same report discusses the condition under which foodstuffs are stored and handled. It leaves no room for doubt as to the need for a better standard of cleanliness in displaying, handling, and storing eatables.

. . . . .

Literature.—Wherever one travels in the wide field of the literature of Scotland one is sure to stumble across references to passages in the Scriptures: the frequency of the references depending largely on the nature of the subject treated. This habit doubtless grew out of the fact that prior to the issues of the Bassandyne Bible in 1576 and 1579 the Latin Vulgate, with its apocryphal books, was in use by those who taught and preached. The constant use of one book, with its strong religious appeal to the heart of man, made a lasting impression on the minds of those who heard and studied it.

However much Scotland gained by the

Union in 1707, one thing may be regarded as almost certain, she has for the most part lost her native tongue. This began long before that eventful period by the introduction of the English Bible (the Wyclif version) and the invasion of English literature. These influences naturally tended to weaken the use of the vernacular and at the same time strengthen the Teutonic.

The effort which is now being made to bring about a revival of the vernacular is worthy of encouragement. For the history of those eventful days through which our forebears passed will be better understood and appreciated if read in the vernacular than in modern English. There were certain words and phrases then used which were so expressive of the deeds done, that it would be difficult to find equivalents in present-day English speech.

Playing golf one summer day at the Kyles of Bute, I remember my second drive at the first hole landed on a big stone. Instantly my caddie remarked : "Did you see how it stottit ? " What feelings the mention of that word aroused could only be appreciated by a native of the country. If the caddie had said : "Did you see how it rebounded," I would have readily responded, but would not have experienced any unusual emotion. It would certainly be to the advantage of the youth in Scotland to know both languages so that they could adjust themselves to particular occasions and circumstances. At present one could confidently say that there are very few young people of the present generation in Scotland who could read understandingly Dr P. Hately Waddell's translation of *The Psalms frae Hebrew until Scottis*. Here is a verse from the twenty-third Psalm :

Na : tho' I gang thro the dead-mirk dail
    e'en thar sal I dread nae skaithin ;
    for yerself are nar-by me ; yer
    stok and yer stay haud me
    baith fu cheerie.

The Educational Life

Improving our English speech has meant in many cases forsaking our mother-tongue, and that often involves losing one's individuality. Owing to Scotland's proximity to England, especially that part of Scotland where the Lowland tongue is most in evidence, it will always be difficult to maintain her individuality. England's greater population and her much greater output of literature and almost everything else puts the smaller country pretty much at the mercy of the bigger one. The process of Anglicisation is almost an everyday matter. Nowhere is it more glaring than in a certain well-to-do class of Scots people who have imbibed and become strangely addicted to the affected and unnatural use of the English tongue, almost out-cockneying anything I have ever heard in the heart of London. The word " black " was pronounced " blek," and " glad " pronounced as though it was spelt " gled," and so on.

To counteract the tendency of being swallowed up by the larger entity, Scotland should hold fast to whatever is distinctive in her national character, and what is more distinctive than language ? One way to do that is to support the movement for a revival of the mother-tongue, which for richness, expressiveness, and melody is perhaps unequalled. The home, the public school, Burns' Clubs, and other like agencies can all assist in promoting the study of the old Scottish language and literature.

Scottish poets and writers have done an immense service to the people in stimulating appreciation of national scenery. More than in most people I have met, the Scots show an unusual affection for nature.

My own reading of the best recent fiction by Scottish writers confirms what was said by a reviewer of *The Grey Coast*, that " it is no exaggeration to state that this novel will not suffer by comparison

with any of its kind in the whole range
of Scottish literature."

.   .   .   .   .

Music.—Every Scotsman has a rich and
goodly heritage in the songs and poems
composed by her sons and daughters. So
sterling, so true are they to human life
that generation after generation find them
knit as it were into their souls. It is
not too much to say that the melody and
the words of Scottish songs are to the
spirit of the people what a cheery fire on
a cold winter's night is to the body.

The songs of Scotland have given her
a wide reputation, so wide that one
naturally expects when in this land to
find every one musical and nearly every
one taking advantage of the opportunity
given for singing. But my own observa-
tion leads me to the opposite view. I
did not find the young people as keenly
alive to the old songs or as responsive to
Church or community singing as I thought
they would be.

Scotland through American Eyes

I heard a preacher announce the first six verses of the ninety-fifth metrical psalm in which the first two lines read :

> O come, let us sing to the Lord :
> come, let us ev'ry one.

By way of getting a full response from the congregation he added : "Note what the psalm says, 'every one.'" The response may have been better for the reminder, but it was anything but satisfactory—many never opening their mouths. I spoke of this particular case to four intelligent young Scotsmen at an hotel on the East Coast of Scotland where I was spending a few days, and they were inclined to attribute much of the Scotsman's silence in singing to self-consciousness.

We are told that it was during the Golden Age (1424–1542) that "Scotland reached the zenith of her fame in music." Robert Fergusson the poet comes much later than this—born in 1750—but it is interesting to note what he says *On the Death of Scots Music*. The last verse reads :

> O Scotland ! that could yence afford
> To bang the pith of Roman sword
> Winna [1] your sons, wi joint accord,
> To battle speed.
> And fight till music be restored,
> Which now lies dead.

Whatever may be said about the age that Fergusson lived in, it is far from the actual state of music to-day. Backward as music is in some of the remote parts of Scotland (for the tuning-fork has not altogether gone out of use), most of the congregational singing will compare favourably with what is rendered in the churches in the United States. I have never witnessed more attentive listeners to vocal and instrumental music nor more appreciative audiences than in Scotland. It would be a colossal loss, not only to the country itself but to the whole world, if

[1] Will not.

there was the least slackening of interest in musical culture in Scotland. Music is a mighty spiritual power in driving away greyness and dreariness. We need it in order to do our best work. Burns, in one of his letters, says: " I never hear the loud solitary whistle of the curlew in a summer noon or the wild rustling cadence of a troop of grey plovers in an autumnal morning, without feeling an elevation of soul." The day is coming when all industry will be attuned to music. That day can be hastened by parents taking a real interest in the musical life of the children in the home and school.

． ． ． ． ．

The Recreational Life.—One has only to look at the daily newspapers in order to get some idea as to the popularity of sports and to note the unusual and increasing amount of space devoted to reporting the many different games. How the editor of an important newspaper looks at cricket may be judged from the following reference. In July 1926 the Australian cricket team played England at Manchester. In reporting the interest and score *The Glasgow Herald* put the news on the editorial page. There can be no question as to sports of one kind and another filling a large place in the minds of the Scottish people. There are those who believe it is much overdone. As a rule the people who take that position are in the minority and perhaps belong to the class who never indulged in outdoor play. On the other hand, there are those who see in games a fine healthy interest and welcome change from work that is often monotonous and machine-like.

It would, we think, be difficult to offset by logic or facts the physical, mental, and moral benefits derived from nearly all outdoor games. In community and international life they have been a distinct factor in promoting goodwill and fellowship. This much can be said with the utmost confidence that Britain need never fear a revolution similar to what took place in France in 1789, nor need she ever be afraid of Bolshevism taking root in this land of law and liberty and sportsmanship. My basis for this confidence rests entirely on the nature of the people themselves. Fair play is an outstanding characteristic of the British people, and fair play is what is demanded in all the varied sports and pastimes.

An additional word ought to be said. Play is a means to an end. If the end is abundant health and fitness to discharge one's duties in all the relations of life, then a moderate amount of play is all to the good.

THE POLITICAL LIFE

CHAPTER VI

THE POLITICAL LIFE

Rights spring from duties fulfilled.

THE Anglicisation of Scotland has gone on apace before and after the Union of 1707. Long before that time the English language had taken a firm grip on the people, the natural consequence being a lessening of the use of the mother-tongue. This was almost unavoidable, but the fact remains that to lose one's language is in the main to lose one's life. The national life of Scotland is to-day far from robust. She has suffered because the larger entity (England), in a large measure, controls her domestic affairs. Whatever view one takes of this matter, it will, we think, be generally admitted that they do not receive the attention

K   145

they ought to in the British Parliament. There is no valid reason why Scottish affairs should be managed and directed from England. Under date of 14th April 1927 *The Glasgow Herald* said, " Scottish Home Rule is not a live issue in Scotland to-day." If the writer of this editorial were called in question for some proof of that assertion he would doubtless take refuge in the word " live." When all the aspects of the question are carefully considered, there is but one conclusion. If it is not a live question it ought to be, and without further delay. Would there be any occasion for an utterance like the following if Scotland were allowed to manage her own affairs, just as a business man or corporation would manage the affairs entrusted to them ? The article from which the quotation is taken referred to the fact that between Parish, Municipal, and Government the rates had become almost unbearable, then added : " What the country really needs is a

Mussolini who will cut down national expenditure on something more than a pettifogging scale." [*The Scottish Country Life* for April 1927.] What an admission this is of the inability of the British Parliament to deal with a matter of this nature. No, a usurper, a dictator can never take the place of the ratepayer without weakening the social and political structure, for the whole principle of life is based on giving as well as receiving, on duties performed as well as rights conceded.

While I write there is the Greenock Burgh Extension Bill up for consideration before the House of Commons Select Committee on Private Bills. The proposal is for the Amalgamation of Greenock, Gourock, and Port Glasgow, and the Committee is comprised of four men, three Conservatives and one Socialist, all representing constituencies in England. It would be difficult to conceive of anything more archaic than this, men in

England determining the affairs of Scotland. " In the case of the extension of Edinburgh to include Leith the expenses were £51,771. The last Glasgow Boundaries extension cost the municipal ratepayers £46,308. . . ." Dunoon, which has a population of less than fifteen thousand, had to go " to the House of Commons to get powers to increase its pier dues from 1d. to 2d."

It is inconceivable that a people as intelligent as the Scottish are should be so indifferent concerning the management of their own affairs. Augustine Birrell, who represented Fifeshire for seven years, said, in 1896 : " There is no need to be ashamed of the old Scots Parliament (which they had until 1707). It passed laws of unrivalled brevity and perfect intelligibility, a now lost art. Scotland owes ' more to its old Parliament than it yet does to the United Parliament.' "

Speaking of the differences between England and Scotland as to law, religion,

education, etc., Birrell says : " I never
knew an English member, unless he was
by birth a Scotsman, who ever took, or
pretended to take, the least trouble to
understand a Scotch Bill . . . they vote
as they are told by party managers."

The House of Commons consists of
615 members, of whom England returns
492, Wales 36, Scotland 74, and Ireland
13. That makes 541 members outside
of Scotland as against 74 representing
Scotland, who practically take little or
no interest in Scottish affairs. This can
scarcely be called a square deal.

The old bogey of " expensive official-
dom," and the fear of Socialism dominat-
ing a Scottish Parliament, are born of a
distrust of the people. The moment that
canker begins little progress is possible.

Worse than any change in the economic
and social structure of the country is the
over anxiety, the harbouring of fear, on
the part of many people, lest the change
brings loss and disaster. That is not

the way out of the fog. One wants to face the situation with courage, faith, and hope.

See what has happened in the British Parliament since 1874, when two Labour members made their first appearance. Now they number twenty-five out of a total of seventy-four for the whole of Scotland, and they have been fortunate in having a taste of power. This is a tremendous change in a little over fifty years. It was a change that was inevitable, and, like many other reforms, was accentuated by the World War.

That a great industrial community such as we find in the Clyde Valley should be represented in Parliament by men who are thinkers and acquainted at first hand with the conditions and needs of that section of the country is so obvious that one does not need to elaborate. Now that the Labour Party has identified itself with Socialism, what may we expect ? The party represents to-day discordant elements arising from marked differences in policy which may be difficult to fuse. What Socialism is to one section of the party is altogether too conservative a dose for another element, and so on. Generally speaking, they all want a society totally different from that which is characteristic of modern industrial civilisation. " A new order of society resting on a new economic basis and emphasising new ethical values." Well, when one calmly considers the matter, that is just what has taken place, notably within the last fifty years, and the process has not by any means slackened. Note the striking changes in the extension of the franchise. In 1868 a Scottish Franchise Act gave the burgh franchise on the same terms as England, that is, to all male householders who paid poor rates. The country qualification was £14 a year for occupiers. In 1884 a Reform Bill was passed which practically granted household suffrage both in towns and country. Now it is proposed to give the right to vote to all women of twenty-one years of age and over. Labour was never more fully represented municipally and nationally than now ; and working conditions, remuneration, and a desire on the part of employers and employees to co-operate were never better than to-day. There is less repression and oppression in every branch of industry than ever before. With a wider diffusion of knowledge things can never remain as they are. The existing economic and social order will in the course of time give place to something different. The movement, however, will be in accord with the spirit and temper of the people, evolutionary and not revolutionary.

Could any better illustration of the temper of the British people be given than what happened during the more than six months of coal stoppage. Think of the fortitude and the loyalty of over a million men to their leaders, and during that long period, save a few trivial assaults, the conduct of the strikers was acknowledged to be exemplary.

I witnessed a football match between England and Scotland in April 1927, in Glasgow. It was estimated that something like 110,000 persons were present. I must confess I never was in a more orderly, good-natured crowd, and I have been in many. It is almost unthinkable that such a multitude, familiar with the rules of the game, could ever be induced —that is, in any large number—to favour violent or revolutionary methods. The soil of Britain is not congenial for the planting of Communism or Bolshevism. For years I have shared the convictions expressed by Lord Haldane (9th October 1926): " They (the British people) need never be afraid of Bolshevism in a country like ours." What they have to fear is the results which may follow stagnation.

The extreme political views held by a considerable number to-day is nothing short of a reaction to the strong individualism of former days. In Scotland to-day the disposition of a considerable number is to look to the State to provide the wherewithal, as though the State had unlimited power. We should not look in vain to the State to recognise, guarantee, and protect the rights and liberties inherent in personality. The State should not be asked to do for the individual what the individual can in most cases do for himself. No kind of government can rise higher and be better than what the individual is. Plan and reform as a government may, the millennium will not come that way. We will understand a little better the times in which we live when we understand the ego. The individual must be brought to see that health and wealth are the offspring of skill, initiative, industry, resourcefulness, self-restraint, and honour. Only by cultivating and developing soul qualities can the individual and society be kept alive and healthy.

The Political Life

As one watches the progress made in the building of a nation, two things stand out clearly, the waning of the power of the sword of steel and the augmenting of the power of the sword of the spirit. It was this spirit that gave to Scotland her independence and freedom, and it is this spirit which will be her mainstay in the days to come. The other is the dwindling rule of the few and the increasing rule of the many. This is as it should be, for no government can ever be satisfactory or endure that does not finally rest on government of the people, by the people, and for the people.

·   ·   ·   ·   ·

The Land Question.—One of the unforgettable experiences in my trip through a portion of French Morocco was starting at daybreak on a January morning from Casablanca for Marakeesh. We had just made a slow exit from the hotel to the bus, when suddenly a strange feeling came over me. The atmosphere seemed to be charged with stillness. The nearness and brightness of the stars was indeed a salutation. We had only gone a few miles in our conveyance when I noticed a shepherd leading his flock of sheep. He was in search of green pastures and waters of rest for his flock, but from all that I could see of the surrounding country most of the land was bare and stony. The whole scene was a reminder of nomadic times when individuals and tribes went hither and thither in search of food for their cattle. This shepherd in the twentieth century was practically doing what Abraham and Lot did over four thousand years ago.

When we pass from the nomadic stage to settled life it is a departure from the common ownership of land to the land portioned among families. The process continues to still larger groups and naturally varies in different countries. In Scotland the feudal system of society came into being in the twelfth century. Under this system the whole land in Scotland " is held either directly under the crown, or indirectly either as vassal to some one who holds immediately from the crown, or as sub-vassal in a more subordinate degree." The system could scarcely be otherwise than characterised by intense individualism. From the King downward it is dependence on a superior. This superior would give title to the land in return for military service and the rendering of certain dues. To-day we are told the land is " held and farmed by the landowner and the farmer, the landowner supplying the capital and getting on an average not more than 2 per cent. for the money."

Now that land reform is one of the leading questions in Britain, the people should know that there is a fundamental distinction, at common law, between property in land and property in goods. " Ownership of land is never absolute, while the ownership of goods is never anything but absolute."

Another equally important point is what was brought out in the course of an address by Professor J. W. Gregory of the University of Glasgow : " No nation has made the land it occupies, or has the right to prevent its adequate use. No nation in our fast-filling earth has the right to adopt a dog-in-the-manger policy regarding land."

Whatever view one takes of the land question in Scotland this much is clear, the right use of the land is of the first importance to every country. Important not only from the food standpoint but also from the health point of view. The fact is, there is no industry like tilling the soil for lessening the plague of un-employment and keeping men fit.

In Scotland agriculture is still an important industry. Every now and then we hear it said or we read in the newspapers that Scotland is a highly industrialised country, and that agriculture, because of the very limited area, is a sort of appendage. It is quite true that the percentage of cultivated area is only 24·2, and that the agricultural returns for Scotland (4th June 1927) shows that the arable land acreage in Scotland has reached the lowest point ever recorded. Further, the area under permanent grass is steadily increasing. " It may be said that Scotland, for the present at least, is diminishing in importance as a crop-raising country, and advancing as a stock-raising and especially as a sheep-farming country." [*The Scotsman*, 30th August 1927.] These facts alone, however, are the strongest reason why the whole land question should be thoroughly investigated.

An encouraging feature of the perplexing problem is that there are at least a few men who are alive to the gravity of the situation, and are able to contribute some helpful material. In *The Courier* and *Advertiser* (Dundee) for 31st August

1927 there is an article on "Modern Conditions — What the Farmer Needs," by J. Moffat Scott of Arbroath, that is worth noting. Summarised, his points are : (1) There is no need for direct government assistance ; (2) It is a question as to whether the system of subsidising the factory instead of the farmer direct is a sound one ; (3) It is a fact that over 55 per cent. [1] of the total cost of production in ordinary arable farming is chargeable to power and labour, so that any reduction that can be made on the cost of these items by a more efficient use of power ought to be sought after ; (4) The future of agriculture depends largely upon the pace at which it becomes industrialised ; (5) One of the mediums which can benefit our industry to the greatest extent is the use of electric power. Here is where a government well-disposed towards agriculture can be of

[1] In some sections of the country it is said to be 40 to 45 per cent.

the greatest possible service; (6) The conservatism of the average Scottish farmer is a hindrance to the development of the co-operative spirit; (7) Specialising in branches of agriculture; (8) Government establishing demonstration farms where agriculture on an extensive scale could be seen.

In this connection an illuminating article on " Farmers since the Days of Noah," in *The National Geographic Magazine* for April 1927, is heartily commended for careful consideration. Of course there is only one big country in the world with which this ancient date could be associated—China.

The Chinese believe that whenever cultivation is possible it should be intensive and not an inch wasted. Some of their rice " fields are no larger than a small room." The claim is often made that the millions of acres of deer areas and grouse moors in Scotland, largely given over to sports, is unfit for anything else. We are inclined to think the Chinese would find it fit for something more.

Industrial Scotland has not begun to realise how dependent we are on the land for our daily sustenance and comfort. " We have only in this country a few weeks of food supplies, and during the War [1914–18] we found out how quickly we could get near starvation point." [Mr Bridgeman, First Lord of the Admiralty, 12th August 1927.]

Industries, like shipbuilding, may in the course of time be obliged to change the centre of their activities in order to get in closer touch with the raw material required, but the basic industry, agriculture, is something that is always with us, and when the land is considerately treated it will be a country's best asset. The detached way in which we look at industry is harmful. Rightly viewed it should be considered an organism in which each and all the parts are vitally related, interdependent.

162

THE SOCIAL LIFE

CHAPTER VII

THE SOCIAL LIFE

Always in your darkest hours
Strive to remember the brightest.
                    J. P. RICHTER

IN making any estimate or passing any
judgment on social conditions as they are
to-day compared with half a century ago
it is only reasonable to take into account
some of the disquieting things which
afflict society from time to time. While
these should be regarded seriously and
attended to thoughtfully they should not
be considered a sign of decline, for just
as individuals have their sicknesses, so
society has afflictions arising out of its
own nature. These may be a prolonged
coal-stoppage, or unemployment on a
large scale, or it may take some form of

propaganda foreign to the institutions of the particular country where it is active.

Figures do not always tell the whole story. For example, we find in the Annual Report of the Prison Commissioners for Scotland for the year 1926, " That the numbers committed to prison last year show an increase—the total number of commitments having been 17,690 as compared with 15,802 in 1925. . . . A considerable proportion of this increase in the number of commitments was doubtless due to the unfortunate labour troubles which occurred during the year. Some of the offences for which persons were committed to prison were directly traceable to these troubles."

Notwithstanding occasional ailments (if they are not too grievous), changes for the better do come to pass in countries where law is respected.

We think it is beyond dispute that a decided change for the better has taken place in the outward circumstances and character of the people. Everywhere one goes in this land of romance it is very gratifying to note how much better the people are attired. Housing conditions are steadily improving, and there are more and better facilities for outdoor recreation.

Half a century ago all letter writing in the commercial and professional world was done in long hand, and the deliveries of all orders for articles of almost any description were done by message boys or men. There were no telephones, no radio, no picture-houses, no gramophones, no motor cars, no aeroplanes, no submarines, no wireless, and practically none of the modern appliances or inventions such as we have to-day. This may not be all clear gain, for all modern appliances are not always used judiciously, but the advantages unmistakably lie on the side of the present rather than the past.

One of the greatest improvements during recent years is the important, although much belated, work which is being done to clear the slum areas in the large cities. In 1923 the Government made a special grant to assist the local authorities in clearing slum areas and building new houses for displaced tenants. A writer in *The Glasgow Herald*, December 1926, said : " Glasgow's slums are not surpassed anywhere for their wretchedness ; they contain a hotch-potch mixture of races ; and the general standard of housing is so low that one out of every two persons one passes in the streets of Glasgow is living more than two to a room."

Some testimony given by medical men before a committee of inquiry into the city improvement scheme promoted by the Glasgow Corporation is pertinent at this point. The conditions described are in certain areas of the east end of Glasgow : " Witness said that in one house of one room were three adults and three children, and in another seven adults. In another property, he added, the plaster of the

walls was bulging and broken, the wood-
work of the floor was gaping, and the
tenants complained of bugs and rats."
Following this witness was a Sanitary
Inspector who said : " . . . that in
one two-apartment house occupied by
six adults and three children there was
no proper water-closet or washing-house
accommodation. On the ground floor of
another building," witness further observed, " there was a one-apartment house
of 1000 cubic feet occupied by nine
people—five adults and four children. It
was entered through a short dark lobby,
and the property was infested with bugs
and rats."

It took Calvinistic Scotland a long time
to wake up to the matter of bringing
more sunshine, better hygienic conditions
into the lives of men, women, and children.
The religious forces in Scotland have been
slower than the educational authorities
to recognise the need of ministering to
the whole life of the individual. " Ye

have the poor always with you," was said of an age and of conditions entirely different from our own. Who wants to be in that category now? The whole struggle (particularly among western nations) is to get out of poverty just as quickly as possible. Scotland still suffers from that condition, but nothing as compared with fifty years ago. There are those who believe that it was out of her poverty that she developed some of her best qualities. Be that as it may, we must recognise that poverty cuts the other way also, for there are many who fail to survive the things incident to poverty. After all, every good quality has its own attraction and reward.

Notwithstanding a long period of depressed trade and high taxation, it is gratifying to find the people of the old land true to one of their strong characteristics—thrift. There is urgent need for the exercise of this quality in the matter of public expenditure. Over fifty years ago (1870–71) the population of the city of Glasgow was assessed at a little over 10s. per head. " To-day they are called upon to pay an average of over £3 per head."

The term " bonnie " as applied to Scotland is not descriptive of its scenery. " Bonnie " may properly be applied to a lassie, but when we come to recall the ruggedness and grandeur of Scotland's mountain ranges and countless hills, the charm and variety of its glens and lochs, another word or phrase that will lift the whole panorama into its unique place in the world of nature is needed.

> Lovest thou mountains great,
> Peaks to the clouds that soar,
> Corrie and fell where eagles dwell,
> And cataracts dash evermore ?
>
> Lovest thou green grassy glades,
> By the sunshine sweetly kist,
> Murmuring waves, and echoing caves ?
> Then go to the Isle of Mist ! [1]

---

[1] From the poem " The Isle of Skye," by Alexander Nicolson.

Scotland through American Eyes

There is a wealth of grandeur in the scenery of Scotland that will always appeal to the artist, tourist, and vacationist, and what one sees in the course of a tour in this beautiful land will always remain a pleasant memory.

This memory will be re-enhanced as one recalls the unfailing courtesies extended by almost every person to strangers and visitors in their travels. There is the gentle, reserveful, and obliging spirit accompanied by the gracious expression " Thank you " which sweetens and brightens all journeying. After many excursions into different parts of the country my conclusion is that all of the varied and charming beauty of the land is calling out for better transport facilities and more up-to-date hotels. It would sometimes seem as though old age had set in, in this *wee* land, for some things have all the earmarks of low vitality. When coming back from one of the many well-advertised all-day tours from the city of Glasgow, our conveyance was unable to pass a motor car coming in the opposite direction because the thoroughfare was too narrow. One of the vehicles had to back a short distance to a wider part of the road before they could pass. This, by no means unusual occurrence, took place within thirty miles of the second largest city in Great Britain, and in a land only 274 miles in length, and as for the age of the old country one almost shrinks from mentioning it. We know that Christianity was introduced as far back as the fourth century. Road building is not something remote from Christianity. On the contrary it may be, as it has been, in nearly all lands a direct means of extending its sway. Yet when we come down to the twentieth century there is a deplorable lack of energy, enterprise, and wisdom in the matter of road building. One wonders whether it is because Scotland is in the political grip of England, or whether it is the effect of the old theological teaching, or is it sheer indifference on the part of the people ?

I have been in large towns and cities where there were no first-class hotels. One city in particular, with a population of nearly 170,000, is to-day without the requirements of a good modern hotel. It is not expensive buildings which the traveller demands, but the conveniences and comforts one finds in the best hotels in other countries. The tourist business of Scotland could easily be doubled if more attention was given to the question of better transport facilities and providing modern conveniences in hotels. A country can be extravagant, but it can also be so penurious as to suffer in the tourist competition now so active in all countries.

In the course of my travels in Scotland I always found a good supply of white bread, cakes, and pastries, but it was very rare to find as wholesome bread combinations as one finds in the large cities of America. Here are a few items taken from the luncheon service of a popular restaurant in New York city:

Nut bread with banana and currant jelly.

Fruit bread a la . . . .

Whole wheat gluten bread with beet and egg.

Rye bread combination.

Whole wheat bread with lettuce and chiffonade dressing.

Bran bread with cream cheese and tomato.

We think it will be admitted that the more general use of these breads would be, from the health point of view, beneficial.

What the young men and young women of Scotland need to be reminded of is that there are more opportunities to-day for making a good competency than ever there were. One has to be vigilant in watching for these opportunities and quick to take advantage of them when they do come. We may be quite certain of this, if Scotsmen fail to sense and grasp the needs of present-day life, there are others beyond these confines who will not hesitate a moment to do so. Alert Americans have already demonstrated what can be done in this country in the way of a profitable business, and we are only at the beginning of what may be done if native talent languishes.

.   .   .   .   .

An Experience and Comment.—In this connection the recital of an afternoon's shopping experience in one of the busiest sections of the largest city in Scotland may not be inapt.

While being shaved in one of the best equipped hairdressing establishments I remarked to the barber that the razor he was using was an unusually good one, it went so smoothly over the face. " What make is it ? " I asked. He promptly replied, " Made in Germany." My next call was at a men's outfitters, where I purchased two neckties. I asked the salesman where they were made. He answered, " They used to be made in Dublin, but owing to the heavy duty in the Free State they are now being made in Belfast." From this shop I went to my tailor to " try-on " a suit of clothes. Knowing that I was from the other side of the Atlantic he was anxious that the fit would be in every way satisfactory. Before we were through with the transaction he made this admission : " There is a touch about the American-made clothes which we are unable to give for some reason."

On my way homeward I was surprised to notice the large number of people in the threepenny and sixpenny shops (or as we call them in America, five and ten cent stores). These stores are growing in number in all industrial centres in Britain and America.

A few days later I visited a hardware

shop to purchase a razor. I asked for the best they had and immediately there was shown me one " Made in Germany," which I purchased. Taken collectively these different experiences gave me the material for some reflection. My first thought was the same thing might be experienced in any country, for no country is exempt from foreign influence and trade. There lingered, however, another thought. Is it possible that there are certain lines of business which Scotland is capable of doing that may be slipping from her ? Whatever the answer may be, this one thing is absolutely certain, that there never was a time in this economic and highly competitive age when Scotland needed to remember the well-known line

"Now's the day and now's the hour"

to produce and market what she can do best.

During my study of conditions in

The Social Life

Scotland I have come across such phrases as " The Americanisation of Europe," " The Americanisation of England " (of course that particular writer meant Britain). There can be no question as to this invasion. Charles M. Schwab, Chairman of the Board of the Bethlehem Steel Corporation, said, Dec. 16th, 1927, " To-day, with five per cent. of the people of the world, we are doing half the world's business." From a highly reputable source the following is taken : " America and things American are an obsession in Europe to-day. Our dances, our songs, our theatres, our sports, our books, our politics, our laws, our life, are studied and discussed, analysed and imitated as never before. Europe is being Americanised." [1] What lies behind this invasion is the tremendous productive power of American industry. Those who only see America as a nation of

[1] By J. W. Wise in *The Century Magazine*, January 1928.

money-makers do not see her best side, nor do they see what underlies their prosperity, initiative, enterprise, energy, and idealism. At heart America is religious after its own best conceptions of life. One reason why the American has been looked upon as a dollar hunter is that he has been more successful at the game than most people, and in the game he has been peculiarly favoured by climate and natural resources, which have in turn brought together a huge population.

.   .   .   .   .

Woman's New Era.—Woman's place in the world has undergone a striking change during the last thirty years, but more especially so since the World War. The world has at last discovered the true worth of womanhood.

> Woman, for centuries
> Held to one little round,
> The prisoner of a blind
> Master, and close confined

The Social Life

To household ministries :
In thy soul, too, was found
As large a love as his,
A sympathy as keen,
A purity as fine,
Courage and strength and brain
Of which the world had need,
But all to one worn, narrow path compelled ;
Or reaching out in dubious way
To influence thy master, and to sway
His world that was by thy birth-throes upheld.[1]

No longer is she restricted to " one worn, narrow path." Maude Royden tells of an experience when she preached in a Presbyterian Church in Scotland. She says, " Well do I remember the way in which I was ordered about. Not being familiar with the service I asked the minister at what point I should go into the pulpit. He told me that I need not be anxious, as he had directed the verger to come and fetch me. The verger interpreted his orders as follows : he led me

[1] From a poem entitled " Vision," by George R. Malloch (1920).

to my seat in the church, leant over the desk in front of me and hissed into my ear, ' Ye'll no stir, till I fetch ye.' " [1]

From a subordinate to an almost equal position with man she has worthily won her way. The theory that might is right has gone for ever. It is right that is mighty and enduring. Now and then it is asserted that it is impossible for a man or woman to follow two vocations at the same time. But what are the many women to do who are confronted with the economic situation, the most pressing of all situations in nearly every country? What has come to pass particularly during the last twenty years is this, women have demonstrated their fitness to fill responsible positions in the different occupations they have thus far entered.

.   .   .   .   .

The Temperance Movement.—The growth of the temperance sentiment in Scotland has been notable during the

[1] From *The British Weekly*, 11th November 1926.

past fifty years. This growth may be largely ascribed to a policy of substitution and restriction, or we may look at the progress from an educational point of view. The policy or programme of giving the public something better than the public-house has proved to be more effective than a policy of subtraction or prohibition. For example, the recreational facilities provided by towns and cities have been of untold benefit to the young and middle-aged, yes, and to some of the older folks. Football pitches, cricket grounds, lawn tennis courts, bowling and putting greens by the hundreds, a number of fine municipal golf courses and public parks, are to be seen in almost every part of the country. These are all of a positive and constructive educational character. The multiplication of tea restaurants and coffee-rooms in almost every part of the largest cities and towns have also played a part in reducing the consumption of alcoholic beverages.

To-day the thought and feeling of the public on the liquor question may be fairly reflected in what took place at a meeting of the Corporation of Glasgow on 7th April 1927. A motion was presented by a member of the Council to rescind the ban on alcoholic refreshments at Corporation functions. The motion read: " That the resolution adopted by the Corporation on 19th October 1925, that no wines, spirits, or other alcoholic liquors be provided at any function held under the auspices of the Corporation, be rescinded." When the division was taken twenty-six voted for the motion and fifty-nine against.

.   .   .   .   .

Population.—People interested in the welfare of their own country as a rule like to know something about those who live in it. In the year 1901, 3,120,241, or 69·77 of the population lived in towns ; towns being reckoned on the basis of 2000 inhabitants and upwards. In that

year the number engaged in industrial occupations was, males 878,446, and females
319,049, or a total of 1,197,495.

Owing to the rapid increase of the
Roman Catholic population in Scotland
during the last twenty years a new factor
in social life has come to the front. Going
as far back as two years before the Union
in 1707, when the population was supposed
to have been 1,000,000, there were said
to be 160 Catholics in Edinburgh, 5 in
Leith, and 12 in Glasgow. The number
of Catholics in the country about the
year 1779 has been estimated at from
20,000 to 30,000. That number, of course,
would not cause any alarm. It is what
has taken place in recent years that
has brought about what many think is
a serious national, as well as religious,
problem. We find that in 1923 the whole
Catholic population was reckoned at over
600 priests, over 450 churches, and about
600,000 adherents. The second annual
report of the Scottish Churches Council

gives the following figures : The population of Scotland in 1921 was 4,882,288, an increase of 121,394 since 1911. It appears from this report that there are about 30,000 Jews in Scotland, of whom about 21,000 are in Glasgow. It is estimated that there are about 640,000 Roman Catholics in Scotland at the present time.

Five times in thirty years the population of Scotland has been larger than it is to-day. The estimated population of Scotland for the year 1926 is 4,903,300. The years 1910, 1919, 1920, 1922, and 1923 were slightly in excess of the year 1926.[1]

From the Appendix No. XVI. of the *Annual Report of the Prison Commissioners for Scotland* for the year 1926, the religious persuasions and nationalities of convicted prisoners, etc., received during the past year are given. Without detailing the

[1] Most of the figures given above are taken from *Chambers's Encyclopædia*, 1927.

particular prisoners, sex and age, they simply give the grand total of two of the largest religious persuasions and nationalities. Presbyterians 9062, Roman Catholics 6080, Scottish 11,495, Irish 3591, including both sexes. Then, again, figures are often quoted without taking into consideration factors and forces of the first importance. These may be found where there is a greater diversity of races and nationalities, where conditions are different, and where there are more opportunities for crime, as is the case in the United States. In Appendix IX. of the above *Report* the number of murders in Scotland is only six, attempts to murder three, and culpable homicides eleven, making a total of twenty. Suppose we put alongside of this a brief statement of crime in the United States for the year 1926 this is what it yields. The combined homicide death-rate in 118 leading cities was 10·1 per 100,000. The city of Chicago, with a population of 2,701,705, according to the census of 1920, had a murder death-rate of 16·7 for the year 1926, New York City 5·7, and Philadelphia 8·6. When all the facts are duly considered Scotland may be justly proud of the low record of the crimes under review.

.   .   .   .   .

Fences.—One of the striking differences between Great Britain and America is to be found in the use of fences enclosing houses and buildings. In Britain there is the high iron fence or iron fence and wall combined, or simply the high stone or concrete wall. In addition to this common practice one will sometimes see a threefold fence in one plot : a stone wall, an iron fence on the wall, and a metal screen inside covering the iron fence. Further, one will occasionally notice a wooden fence on the top of a stone wall. In the United States it is a rare thing to find a high wall or iron railing enclosing a house or public building. The common practice is the open lawn or garden in front of the house, leaving an unobstructed view of both from the street.

Speaking before the Glasgow Rotary Club on 26th July 1927, the Rev. Dr J. R. P. Sclater of Toronto, and formerly of the New North U.F. Church, Edinburgh, said : " In Toronto there were no garden fences, no gates or city walls, but the life there was just as rich and cultivated as at Gilmorehill [Glasgow] or in the sacred shades of Edinburgh University." As one walks along the roads and streets in the residential parts of Scotland, the thing most observable is the cold and inhospitable fence shutting out the view of carefully and often lavishly planned gardens. In order to get a glimpse of the dazzling colourings and the great variety of the flowers, one has in most cases to peer through an iron fence or strain the neck to look over a forbidding wall. Flowers have a modicum of feeling, but after that they are helpless, so some one has to interpret or at least come near what they would say if they possessed the gift of speech. Would it not be something like this :

We have a mission in this world of ours to give what we are. We can give in our brief lives beauty and variety, brightness and fragrance, and food for the bees. Why lessen our ministry by what is not beautiful nor bright nor fragrant —the cold bleak fences ?

Travel where you will through this land of so many well-designed gardens crowded with flowers of rich hues, one will invariably find the homes of all classes enclosed by a wall or iron fence or hedge. British horticulture has attained a high and enviable position, but it can go still higher by suggesting and educating the public to something that will take the place of the present inharmonious fence enclosing garden spaces.

The attitude of the vast majority towards the flowers in the open gardens would be much the same as their attitude towards the books on the shelves in the public libraries. As a rule it is only the exceptional type of person which we have to fear, and, to such, fences are by no means a deterrent. It is just as easy for members of this type to climb a fence or scale a wall as it is to mutilate or annotate a book taken from the public library. In the public squares in Britain where there are flowers and practically no fences it is a rare thing to see anyone touch or take a flower.

The present practice cannot stand the test of right thinking. It is a relic of barbarism and medievalism.

The enclosed garden is a form of exclusiveness, and exclusiveness can never give adequate protection. We live in a very different age from the days when physical prowess counted for worth and for strength. No longer do we look for security in fortresses, castles, and armoury. Our security and peace is to be found in what is basic to human society—trust, goodwill, and justice. It is true that our trust may at times be betrayed, but is it not heartening to think that in the vast majority of cases it is honoured ?

.   .   .   .   .

Humour.—If there is one thing more than another that the American takes especial pride in, it is his sense of humour. He is inclined to underrate other countries in this particular and overrate his own country. Knowing some of the traits which belong to the Scotsman (although he rarely knows from what source they spring) he frequently makes him the butt of his jokes and stories. The following is a fair example : " Order, order," said Satan angrily, " what's the matter ? We don't allow laughter here." " Oh ! it's only a Scotsman who has just seen a joke he heard on earth." Of course, such a story would lack spice and fall flat if, for the Scotsman, one substituted a Chinaman.

Probably few have had a much wider

experience among professional and business men in America and Scotland than the writer. My humble judgment is that Scotsmen are not only humorous but more humorous, after their own fashion, than Americans are after theirs. It is not too much to say that "Humour is the common inheritance of the people." Not long ago I read in a Scottish monthly that " official Scotland is a solemn and somewhat stodgy thing, but Scotland in its unofficial dress is full of genial humour and generous feeling." This tallies with what I have found in my travels throughout Scotland. Unquestionably the wit and humour of both countries is different, so is the spelling of the word " humor " different. When there is similarity it corresponds to like conditions and circumstances, and so in the case of dissimilarity.

Here is a story, taken from a new book entitled *Principal Caird*, by the Rev. Charles L. Warr, that would tickle

N   193

a Scotsman, but would be received by the average American without any pleasurable sensation. It is related that Dr John Caird (who in 1873 became Principal of Glasgow University), while he was minister of a small parish in Scotland, had delivered in the morning one of his stately discourses—usually an hour long. Caird was a man of broad culture, and had a striking personality. One hearer said to another as they left the kirk door, " Was he no graun the day ? " " Aye," was the reply, " but did ye un'erstaun him ? " " Un'erstaun him," exclaimed the first, " I widna presoom." Dr Norman MacLean of Edinburgh, reviewing the above book, said: "It was the magnetic personality expressing itself in majestic oratory that thus swayed even the uncomprehending."

The happy faculty of appreciating a difficult or alarming situation and turning it into one of good humour, especially when it is against his own kin, is characteristic of Scotsmen. While the Government's policy was being attacked in the House of Commons the sudden failure of the lights and other electrical apparatus caused some confusion.

" For the first time in fifty years the order ' let candles be brought in,' was issued by the Speaker. Soon the crowded little chapel-like chamber, in which the House of Commons carries on its affairs, was faintly illumined. The Speaker did not consider the candle-light sufficient to carry on, and ordered an adjournment, but not before John Buchan, famous Scottish novelist and a member of Parliament, had observed that the Scots had buttoned up their coats in the darkness, thereby following out what he called a national instinct." [1]

.   .   .   .   .

National Characteristics. — An intelligent and successful business man in Glasgow said in the course of a conver-

[1] *New York Times*, November 25th, 1927.

sation, " You (that is Americans) may be ahead of us in many things, but there is one thing in which you are not ahead of us—perseverance." This was a modest but very conscious way of expressing what could scarcely be challenged. It was simply affirming the substance of the old Scottish proverbs, " When ae door steeks anither opens," and " He that tholes owercomes." One often hears expressions like " Wha's like us ? " Conversing at the dinner table with a young minister he dropped this remark, " The Scots people have certain opinions about things and we think they are right." Here is part of a prayer which I heard at a Sunday morning service in a large church in Glasgow : " Bless our beloved land. How can we love another land so well."

In *A Study of British Genius*, by Havelock Ellis, he discovered that " in science Scotland stands very high, and in great soldiers stands easily at the head." His

study is based on an examination of the
material found in sixty-nine volumes of
the *Dictionary of National Biography*,
1030 persons of imminent intellectual
ability were selected out of a record of
over 30,000 persons. This fact must be
of interest to Scotsmen everywhere. It is
a most creditable and honourable record,
and may partly account for the measure
of pride common among Scotsmen. We
would like to add to this record Scotland's
many eminent preachers and thinkers.

The religious impulse is more in evidence
in the Scottish people than in most people
I have met with in my travels. We find
him independent, patient, patriotic, and
polemic. His practical bent is more in
evidence than his idealism. A common
attitude of the Scot is his pensiveness;
he will often be seen smoking, deep in
thought, and looking steadily at the
cheery fire. Next to a fortune he loves
and relishes an argument.

During my stay here I have come in

close touch with commercial and professional men; have done an unusual amount of purchasing in the shops, and what has impressed me most was the courtesy and readiness to assist in any way possible. I went into one of the bus offices in Glasgow to find out if the golf courses at a small town about twenty miles from Glasgow were available to visitors on the payment of a fee. A gentleman standing near me overheard the conversation, and at once suggested to the clerk that he could find out by telephoning to a friend of his who lived in the town. He got the needed information promptly and informed me.

Thriftiness, seriousness, and thoughtfulness are characteristics common to the Scot. When we try to get some inkling as to the source of the traits that constitute the Scottish character, we find some at least are connected with conditions and circumstances which have nothing to do with individual effort, such as the physical features of the land and its climate, and still others from the heritage of mixed races. One may feel almost sure in saying there is no such thing as an absolutely pure race. Different races at different periods, prehistoric and historic, have entered into the life of this little land, thus making a composite people. On a close analysis it would, we think, be found that we share some of the qualities common to the Celts, Romans, Teutons, Norse, Norman, and Fleming. National pride to a large extent grows out of the long struggle for independence and an undying admiration for the men who fought so valiantly for their country. Whatever there is of national conceit is an old tribal and natural failing, growing out of a limited historical outlook.

Further, the Scot of to-day is, in some respects, unlike the Scot of fifty years ago. The influences and forces which go to make up his environment are entirely different, hence a somewhat new type of man and woman is inevitable. In this changing world it is of the first importance to Scotsmen to make every effort to conserve whatever is strongest and best in her people.

.   .   .   .   .

Climate and Clothing. — To spend nearly five winter months in Spain and French Morocco, with almost continual sunshine, is a decided contrast to spending the same time, about the same season of the year, in Scotland, where changeable, and, for the most part, rainy weather was experienced. It is fair to say that most people would prefer the sunny climate of Spain or Southern California or Florida, in the United States of America, to the drab and moist weather in Scotland. The people who live in sunny climes long for copious rains, just as those who live where rain is abundant sigh for the genial sun. A question not easily answered is, Do the advantages lie in a land of almost steady sunshine or in a land where

changes and moisture predominate ? Of
this at least we are sure — life is a
continuous struggle, and when we have
nothing to combat, nothing to try our
mettle, a weakening of the physical and
mental fibre ensues. Admitting this to
be fairly correct, it would seem as though
the advantages lie with those who live
in the temperate zone, and with those
who can withstand a rigorous climate.
There is no need, then, to cast envious
eyes on those who live most of the time
in sunny lands. For the tendency there
is to make one soft, whereas in the
northern climes the tendency is in the
opposite direction. In fact, it may be
considered an asset of considerable character value.

Much can be done in Scotland to
make even the drab, dull, depressing
days brighter, bonnier, and blither. The
marked change from sombre to bright
colours in ladies' attire is an admirable
move ; it has a distinct psychological

effect on the days that are cloudy and heavy with moisture.

The matter of the best kind of wearing apparel is still in the making, like life itself. Some useful information in the way of dressing well during the last twenty years or so has been gained and adopted. We have discovered that warmth is not entirely dependent on the amount of clothing one wears, but rather on the condition of the body and proper circulation, and that snug-fitting, or tight-fitting clothes may easily keep out the air which is so essential to health. It is not so many years ago when the number of ounces to the yard for men's woollen suits was something like twenty-two; now it is about seventeen or eighteen in America, and I understand that a change in the same direction has taken place in Scotland. With a suitable, well-ventilated dress or outer garment, made of the lightest and most porous material, the women of Scotland would be the envy

The Social Life

of those in sunny lands, for there are no cosmetics that can equal those of rain and pure air in the great open spaces— these are nature's beauty parlours.

From what has been written of the climate of Scotland one would imagine that something in the nature of an arctic climate took place every winter. Two brief incidents will relate my experience of the winter of 1926–27. On a motor car trip in the middle of January we went from Crieff to Pitlochry, through the Sma' Glen. There we saw, on the hillside, a shepherd with his faithful dog and flock of scattered sheep amid surroundings as beautiful as one would ever see on a June day. On our return trip we noticed two men busy fishing in the River Tay. What did it matter to them if they were over the knees in water so long as the fishing was good! Another experience was this : while taking a walk on the outskirts of Glasgow on Sunday afternoon, 21st February 1927, I experienced one of those delightful surprises that gladdens one's heart. I have always been passionately fond of the lark; he is such a mirthful and inspiring little bird. On this winter's day, just on the border-line of the big city, he was singing like a Galli-Curci and at the same time going

> Higher still and higher
> From the earth thou springest;
> Like a cloud of fire
> The deep blue thou wingest;
> And singing still dost soar, and soaring
> ever singest.[1]

Since some days must be dark and dreary, we must never allow the outward to master the inward climate.

With the planting of more evergreen trees in towns and cities and more attention given to colour in public and private buildings much could be done to dispel the gloominess of many streets.

· · · · ·

[1] From " To a Skylark," by Shelley.

The Social Life

The Larger Outlook. — There are some things which are written so large in the life of humanity as to be beyond dispute. One of them is the futility of the individual attempting to live by and for himself. He is a dependent and interdependent being. He is bound up with the whole, that is, the entire world. This proposition is now a matter of common experience, and while it may not be accepted in some provincial quarters, the unmistakable tendency of our time is toward a world democracy. It is true that much remains to be done before that auspicious day dawns, but we are heartened by the fact that we have seen in our time distances annihilated, isolation made impossible, and a working League of Nations possible.

The removal of all economic barriers between the nations of the world will be a tremendous stride toward world peace and prosperity. The United States of America has forty-eight States, and between each and all there is the freest kind of trading—no internal barriers whatsoever, and no strife nor wars. Europe, which may in the course of time become the United States of Europe, has over a score of custom barriers, which are a constant source of friction. In the cultivation of the international mind, in the building of a world consciousness, Scotland, by virtue of its leading characteristic—religion—is well fitted to lead in the movement for world unity.

INDEX

Scotland through American Eyes